This Timeless Collection
Is Presented To:

_____

On

_____

By

_____

AGELESS
INSPIRATIONS

COMPILED BY
ELLIE BUSHA

Evergreen Communications, Inc.
Ventura, California

Ageless Inspirations

Published by
Evergreen Communications, Inc.
2085-A Sperry Avenue
Ventura, CA 93003
(805) 650-9248

Unless otherwise indicated, Scripture quotations are from the *King James Version* of the Bible. Public domain.

Scripture quotations marked (*NIV*) are from the Holy Bible, New International Version. Copyright © 1973, 1978, 1984 International Bible Society. Used by permission of Zondervan Bible Publishers.

Library of Congress Cataloging-in-Publication Data:

Ageless Inspirations / [compiled by] Ellie Busha.
      p.   cm.
    Includes index.
   ISBN 0-926284-04-5
   1. Devotional literature, English   I. Busha, Ellie, 1929-
BV4801.A44   1990
242—dc20   90-19569
                                         CIP

99 98 97 96 95 94 93 92 91 90   9 8 7 6 5 4 3 2 1

Printed in the United States of America

Much of the material in this book is under public domain and, in some cases, the authors are unknown. However, the author and publisher have sought to locate and secure permission to reprint copyrighted material in this book. If any such acknowledgments have been inadvertently omitted, the publisher would appreciate receiving the information so that proper credit may be given in future printings.

Dedicated
to my husband, Don,
and to my family
for their loving support
during the months
of compiling this book,
and to Clint and Mary,
whose help and encouragement
have brought about
its publication.

Contents

Preface

Preface

Ageless Inspirations is a compilation of works by a host of writers, many whose names you will recognize. Some of the authors are from the pages of history, others are more contemporary, but all have contributed to the inspirational classics we have come to know and to love.

Many years ago, Ellie Busha began her collection of favorite poems, prayers, quotations, Scripture verses, and hymns, recording them in a little brown notebook. Soon that notebook became filled and overflowing, so she added other notebooks, large envelopes, and eventually a filing cabinet to hold her treasury. From her files, then, comes *Ageless Inspirations*.

You can find these literary gems scattered among several volumes, but this book combines them into one timeless collection.

Included you'll find those pieces that have come down to us through the ages and that are the most familiar. We know you'll enjoy reading, and rereading, the over 400 entries, from Scripture verses to poems and well-known quotations, from favorite hymns to prayers, both from the Bible and from the hearts of men and women.

Some of the material was gleaned from greeting cards, old magazine and newspaper clippings, bookmarks, and the like, so in many cases the original writer is unknown. We have included names and dates whenever possible.

For your convenience in finding your favorite pieces, an index has been included, listing titles in bold print and first lines in italics. In addition, we have added pages at the end of each section for you to fill in your own favorites.

Ellie Busha is a wife, mother, grandmother, and great-grandmother who makes her home in Fenton, Michigan. She herself is a writer, having composed many poems, devotions, and songs.

We're thankful to Ellie for sharing her collection of favorites with us. And we pray that this book will bless, inspire, and encourage all who read it.

Clint and Mary Beckwith,
Publishers
November 1990

Part One

Treasured Prayers

The Lord's Prayer

Our Father which art in heaven,
Hallowed be thy name.
Thy kingdom come.
Thy will be done
in earth, as it is in heaven.
Give us this day our daily bread.
And forgive us our debts,
as we forgive our debtors.
And lead us not into temptation,
but deliver us from evil:
For thine is the kingdom, and the power,
and the glory, for ever. Amen.

Matthew 6:9-15

Doxology

Praise God, from whom all blessings flow;
Praise Him, all creatures here below;
Praise Him above, ye heavenly host;
Praise Father, Son, and Holy Ghost.
Amen.

Gloria Patri

Glory be to the Father, and to the Son,
And to the Holy Ghost;
As it was in the beginning,
Is now, and ever shall be,
World without end.
Amen, Amen.

Gloria In Excelsis

Glory be to God on high, and on earth peace, good will toward men. We praise thee, we bless thee, we worship thee, we glorify thee, we give thanks to thee for thy great glory, O Lord God, heavenly King, God the Father Almighty.

O Lord, the only-begotten Son, Jesus Christ; O Lord God, Lamb of God, Son of the Father, that takest away the sins of the world, have mercy upon us. Thou that takest away the sins of the world, receive our prayer. Thou that sittest at the right hand of God the Father, have mercy upon us.

For thou only art holy; thou only art the Lord; thou only, O Christ, with the Holy Ghost, art most high in the glory of God the Father. Amen.

The Apostles' Creed

I believe in God the Father Almighty, maker of heaven and earth; And in Jesus Christ his only Son our Lord: who was conceived by the Holy Spirit, born of the Virgin Mary, suffered under Pontius Pilate, was crucified, dead, and buried; the third day he rose from the dead; he ascended into heaven, and sitteth at the right hand of God the Father Almighty; from thence he shall come to judge the quick and the dead.

I believe in the Holy Spirit, the holy catholic Church, the communion of saints, the forgiveness of sins, the resurrection of the body, and the life everlasting. Amen.

The Nicene Creed

I believe in one God: the Father Almighty, maker of heaven and earth, and of all things visible and invisible;

And in one Lord Jesus Christ, the only begotten Son of God: begotten of the Father before all worlds, God of God, Light of Light, very God of very God, begotten, not made, being of one substance with the Father, through whom all things were made; who for us men and for our salvation came down from heaven, and was incarnate by the Holy Ghost of the Virgin Mary, and was made man, and was crucified also for us under Pontius Pilate; he suffered and was buried, and the third day he rose again according to the Scriptures, and ascended into heaven, and sitteth on the right hand of the Father; and he shall come again with glory, to judge both the quick and the dead; whose kingdom shall have no end.

And I believe in the Holy Ghost, the Lord, the giver of life, who proceedeth from the Father and the Son, who with the Father and the Son together is worshiped and glorified, who spake by the prophets. And I believe in one holy catholic and apostolic Church. I acknowledge one baptism for the remission of sins. And I look for the resurrection of the dead, and the life of the world to come. Amen.

Benedictus

Blessed be the Lord God of Israel;
for he hath visited and redeemed his people;
And hath raised up a mighty salvation for us,
in the house of his servant David;
As he spake by the mouth of his holy prophets,
which have been since the world began;
That we should be saved from our enemies,
and from the hand of all that hate us.
To perform the mercy promised to our forefathers,
and to remember his holy covenant;
To perform the oath which he sware to our forefather
Abraham, that he would give us;
That we being delivered out of the hand of our enemies
might serve him without fear;

In holiness and righteousness before him,
    all the days of our life.
And thou, child, shalt be called the prophet of the
Highest: for thou shalt go before the face of the Lord
    to prepare his ways;
To give knowledge of salvation unto his people
    for the remission of their sins,
Through the tender mercy of our God;
    whereby the day-spring from on high hath visited us;
To give light to them that sit in darkness, and in the
    shadow of death, and to guide our feet into
    the way of peace.
Glory be to the Father and to the Son,
    and to the Holy Ghost;
As it was in the beginning, is now, and ever shall be,
    world without end. Amen.

De Profundis

O ut of the depths have I cried unto thee, O LORD.
Lord, hear my voice: let thine ears be attentive to
the voice of my supplications.

If thou, LORD, shouldest mark iniquities, O Lord,
who shall stand?

But *there is* forgiveness with thee, that thou mayest be
feared.

I wait for the LORD, my soul doth wait, and in his
word do I hope.

My soul *waiteth* for the Lord more than they that watch for the morning: *I say, more than* they that watch for the morning.

Let Israel hope in the LORD: for with the LORD *there is* mercy, and with him *is* plenteous redemption.

And he shall redeem Israel from all his iniquities.

Psalm 130

Te Deum

We praise thee, O God; we acknowledge thee to be the Lord.

All the earth doth worship thee, the Father everlasting.
To thee all angels cry aloud; the heavens and all the
powers therein;
to thee cherubim and seraphim continually do cry,
Holy, holy, holy, Lord God of Sabaoth;
heaven and earth are full of the majesty of thy glory.
The glorious company of the apostles praise thee.
The goodly fellowship of the prophets praise thee.
The noble army of martyrs praise thee.
The holy Church throughout all the world doth ac-
knowledge thee;
The Father, of an infinite majesty; thine adorable, true,
and only Son; also the Holy Ghost, the Comforter.
Thou art the King of Glory, O Christ.
Thou art the everlasting Son of the Father.
When thou tookest upon thee to deliver man,
thou didst humble thyself to be born of a virgin.

When thou hadst overcome the sharpness of death,
    thou didst open the kingdom of heaven to all believers.
Thou sittest at the right hand of God,
    in the glory of the Father.
We believe that thou shalt come to be our judge.
    We therefore pray thee, help thy servants,
    whom thou hast redeemed with thy precious blood.
Make them to be numbered with thy saints,
    in glory everlasting.
O Lord, save thy people, and bless thine heritage.
    Govern them, and lift them up forever.
Day by day we magnify thee;
    and we worship thy name ever, world without end.
Vouchsafe, O Lord, to keep us this day without sin.
    O Lord, have mercy upon us, have mercy upon us.
O Lord, let thy mercy be upon us, as our trust is in thee.
    O Lord, in thee have I trusted; let me never be
    confounded.

The Magnificat

My soul doth magnify the Lord,
And my spirit hath rejoiced in God my Saviour.
    For he hath regarded the low estate of his handmaiden:
for, behold, from henceforth all generations shall call me
blessed.
    For he that is mighty hath done to me great things; and
holy *is* his name.

And mercy *is* on them that fear him from generation to generation.

He hath shewed strength with his arm; he hath scattered the proud in the imagination of their hearts.

He hath put down the mighty from *their* seats, and exalted them of low degree.

He hath filled the hungry with good things; and the rich he hath sent empty away.

He hath holpen his servant Israel, in remembrance of *his* mercy;

As he spake to our fathers, to Abraham, and to his seed for ever.

Luke 1:46-55

The Ten Commandments

I. I *am* the LORD thy God. Thou shalt have no other gods before me.

II. Thou shalt not make unto thee any graven image, or any likeness of *any thing* that is in heaven above, or that is in the earth beneath, or that *is* in the water under the earth.

III. Thou shalt not take the name of the LORD thy God in vain.

IV. Remember the sabbath day, to keep it holy.

V. Honour thy father and thy mother: that thy days may be long upon the land which the LORD thy God giveth thee.

VI. Thou shalt not kill.

VII. Thou shalt not commit adultery.

VIII. Thou shalt not steal.
 IX. Thou shalt not bear false witness against thy
neighbour.
  X. Thou shalt not covet...any thing that is thy
neighbour's.

From Exodus 20:3-17

The Beatitudes

B lessed *are* the poor in spirit: for theirs is the kingdom of heaven.

Blessed *are* they that mourn: for they shall be comforted.

Blessed *are* the meek: for they shall inherit the earth.

Blessed *are* they which do hunger and thirst after righteousness: for they shall be filled.

Blessed *are* the merciful: for they shall obtain mercy.

Blessed *are* the pure in heart: for they shall see God.

Blessed *are* the peacemakers: for they shall be called the
children of God.

Blessed *are* they which are persecuted for righteousness'
sake: for theirs is the kingdom of heaven.

Blessed *are* ye, when *men* shall revile you, and persecute
you, and shall say all manner of evil against you
falsely, for my sake.

Rejoice, and be exceeding glad: for great *is* your reward
in heaven: for so persecuted they the prophets which
were before you.

Matthew 5:3-12

Twenty-Third Psalm

The Lord *is* my shepherd; I shall not want.
He maketh me to lie down in green pastures: he leadeth me beside the still waters.

He restoreth my soul: he leadeth me in the paths of righteousness for his name's sake.

Yea, though I walk through the valley of the shadow of death, I will fear no evil: for thou *art* with me; thy rod and thy staff they comfort me.

Thou preparest a table before me in the presence of mine enemies: thou anointest my head with oil; my cup runneth over.

Surely goodness and mercy shall follow me all the days of my life: and I will dwell in the house of the Lord for ever.

Psalm 23

Psalm 8

O LORD our Lord, how excellent *is* thy name in all the earth! who hast set thy glory above the heavens.

Out of the mouth of babes and sucklings hast thou ordained strength because of thine enemies, that thou mightest still the enemy and the avenger.

When I consider thy heavens, the work of thy fingers, the moon and the stars, which thou hast ordained;

What is man, that thou art mindful of him? and the son of man, that thou visitest him?

For thou hast made him a little lower than the angels, and hast crowned him with glory and honour.

Thou madest him to have dominion over the works of thy hands; thou hast put all *things* under his feet:

All sheep and oxen, yea, and the beasts of the field;

The fowl of the air, and the fish of the sea, *and whatsoever* passeth through the paths of the seas.

O LORD our Lord, how excellent *is* thy name in all the earth!

Psalm 91

He that dwelleth in the secret place of the most High shall abide under the shadow of the Almighty.

I will say of the LORD, *He is* my refuge and my fortress: my God; in him will I trust.

Surely he shall deliver thee from the snare of the fowler, *and* from the noisome pestilence.

He shall cover thee with his feathers, and under his wings shalt thou trust: his truth *shall be thy* shield and buckler.

Thou shalt not be afraid for the terror by night; nor for the arrow *that* flieth by day;

Nor for the pestilence that walketh in darkness; nor for the destruction that wasteth at noonday.

A thousand shall fall at thy side, and ten thousand at thy right hand; but it shall not come nigh thee.

Only with thine eyes shalt thou behold and see the reward of the wicked.

Because thou hast made the LORD, which is my refuge, even the most High, thy habitation;

There shall no evil befall thee, neither shall any plague come nigh thy dwelling.

For he shall give his angels charge over thee, to keep thee in all thy ways.

They shall bear thee up in their hands, lest thou dash thy foot against a stone.

Thou shalt tread upon the lion and adder: the young lion and the dragon shalt thou trample under feet.

Because he hath set his love upon me, therefore will I deliver him: I will set him on high, because he hath known my name.

He shall call upon me, and I will answer him: I will be with him in trouble; I will deliver him, and honour him.

With long life will I satisfy him, and shew him my salvation.

A Psalm of Praise

Make a joyful noise unto the LORD, all ye lands.
Serve the LORD with gladness: come before his presence
with singing.
Know ye that the LORD he *is* God: *it is* he that hath
made us, and not we ourselves; *we are* his people, and
the sheep of his pasture.
Enter into his gates with thanksgiving, *and* into his courts
with praise: be thankful unto him, *and* bless his name.
For the LORD *is* good; his mercy *is* everlasting; and his
truth *endureth* to all generations.

Psalm 100

Psalm 121

I will lift up mine eyes unto the hills, from whence
cometh my help.

My help *cometh* from the LORD, which made heaven
and earth.

He will not suffer thy foot to be moved: he that keepeth thee will not slumber.

Behold, he that keepeth Israel shall neither slumber nor sleep.

The LORD *is* thy keeper: the LORD *is* thy shade upon thy right hand.

The sun shall not smite thee by day, nor the moon by night.

The LORD shall preserve thee from all evil: he shall preserve thy soul.

The LORD shall preserve thy going out and thy coming in from this time forth, and even for evermore.

Psalm 150

Praise ye the LORD. Praise God in his sanctuary: praise him in the firmament of his power.

Praise him for his mighty acts: praise him according to his excellent greatness.

Praise him with the sound of the trumpet: praise him with the psaltery and harp.

Praise him with the timbrel and dance: praise him with stringed instruments and organs.

Praise him upon the loud cymbals: praise him upon the high sounding cymbals.

Let every thing that hath breath praise the LORD. Praise ye the LORD.

Benedictions From the Scriptures

The Lord bless thee, and keep thee; The Lord make his face shine upon thee, and be gracious unto thee. The Lord lift up his countenance upon thee, and give thee peace.

Numbers 6:24-26

NOW UNTO HIM that is able to do exceeding abundantly above all that we ask or think, according to the power that worketh in us, Unto him be glory in the church by Christ Jesus throughout all ages, world without end. Amen.

Ephesians 3:20-21

THE GRACE OF our Lord Jesus Christ *be* with you. Amen.

1 Thessalonians 5:28

THE VERY GOD of peace sanctify you wholly; and I *pray God* your whole spirit and soul and body be preserved blameless unto the coming of our Lord Jesus Christ. Amen.

1 Thessalonians 5:23

NOW UNTO HIM that is able to keep you from falling, and to present *you* faultless before the presence of his glory with exceeding joy, To the only wise God our Savior, *be* glory and majesty, dominion and power, both now and ever. Amen.

Jude:24-25

THE GRACE OF the Lord Jesus Christ, and the love of God, and the communion of the Holy Ghost, *be* with you all. Amen.

2 Corinthians 13:14

Lord, what a change within us one short hour
Spent in thy presence will prevail to make!
What heavy burdens from our bosoms take,
What parched grounds refresh as with a shower!
We kneel, and all around us seems to lower;
We rise, and all, the distant and the near,
Stands forth in sunny outline brave and clear;
We kneel, how weak! we rise, how full of power!
Why, therefore, should we do ourselves this wrong,
Or others, that we are not always strong,
That we are ever overborne with care,
That we should ever weak or heartless be,
Anxious or troubled, when with us is prayer,
And joy and strength and courage are with thee!

Richard Chenevix Trench (1807-1886)

More things are wrought by prayer
Than this world dreams of. Wherefore, let thy
  voice
Rise like a fountain for me night and day.
For what are men better than sheep and goats
That nourish a blind life within the brain,
If, knowing God, they lift not hands of prayer
Both for themselves and those who call them friend?
For so the whole round earth is every way
Bound by gold chains about the feet of God.

Alfred Lord Tennyson (1809-1892)

Prayer Is the Soul's Sincere Desire

Prayer is the soul's sincere desire,
Unuttered or expressed;
The motion of a hidden fire
That trembles in the breast.

Prayer is the simplest form of speech
That infant lips can try;
Prayer, the sublimest strains that reach
The Majesty on high.

Prayer is the contrite sinner's voice,
Returning from his ways;
While angels in their songs rejoice
And cry, "Behold, he prays!"

O Thou, by whom we come to God,
The life, the truth, the way,
The path of prayer Thyself hast trod:
Lord, teach us how to pray!

James Montgomery (1771-1854)

If we traverse the world, it is possible to find cities without walls, without letters, without kings, without wealth, without coin, without schools and theaters; but a city without a temple, or that practiseth not worship, prayers, and the like, no one ever saw.

Plutarch (50-120 A.D.)

Proof

If radio's slim fingers can pluck a melody
From night—and toss it over a continent or sea;
If the petalled white notes of a violin
Are blown across the mountains or the city's din;
If songs, like crimson roses, are culled from thin
    blue air—
Why should mortals wonder if God hears prayer?

Ethel Romig Fuller

Favorite Quotations

Prayer is the wing wherewith the soul flies to heaven, and meditation the eye wherewith we see God.

Saint Ambrose (339-397)

ALL THINGS, WHATSOEVER ye shall ask in prayer, believing, ye shall receive.

Matthew 21:22

WITH MEN *IT IS* impossible, but not with God: for with God all things are possible.

Mark 10:27

PRAYER IS THE peace of our spirit, the stillness of our thoughts, the evenness of recollection, the seat of meditation, the rest of our cares, and the calm of our tempest; prayer is the issue of a quiet mind, of untroubled thoughts; it is the daughter of charity and the sister of meekness.

Jeremy Taylor (1613-1667)

IF YOU WOULD never cease to pray, never cease to long for it. The continuance of your longing is the continuance of your prayer.

Saint Augustine (354-430)

PRAYER SHOULD BE the key of the day and the lock of the night.

Thomas Fuller (1608-1661)

PRAYER IS THE contemplation of the facts of life from the highest point of view.

Ralph Waldo Emerson (1803-1882)

A PRAYER IN its simplest definition is merely a wish turned Godward.

Phillips Brooks (1835-1893)

Prayer for Serenity

G od, grant me the serenity to accept the things I
cannot change, courage to change the things I can,
and wisdom to know the difference, living one day at a
time, enjoying one moment at a time, accepting hardship
as a pathway to peace, taking, as Jesus did, this sinful
world as it is, not as I would have it, trusting that You
will make all things right if I surrender to Your will, so
that I may be reasonably happy in this life and supremely
happy with You forever in the next.

Reinhold Niebuhr (1892-1971)

Prayer of Saint Francis of Assisi

L ord,
make me an instrument of Thy peace;
Where there is hatred, let me sow love;
where there is injury, pardon;
where there is doubt, faith;
where there is despair, hope;
where there is darkness, light;
and where there is sadness, joy.
O Divine Master,
grant that I may not so much seek
to be consoled, as to console;
to be understood, as to understand;
to be loved, as to love;

for it is in giving that we receive,
it is in pardoning that we are pardoned,
and it is in dying that we are born
to eternal life.

Saint Francis of Assisi (1182-1226)

Prayer From Psalm 119

Teach me, O LORD, the way of thy statutes; and I shall keep it *unto* the end.

Give me understanding, and I shall keep thy law; yea, I shall observe it with *my* whole heart.

Make me to go in the path of thy commandments; for therein do I delight.

Incline my heart unto thy testimonies, and not to covetousness.

Turn away mine eyes from beholding vanity; *and* quicken thou me in thy way.

Stablish thy word unto thy servant, who *is devoted* to thy fear.

Turn away my reproach which I fear: for thy judgments *are* good.

Behold, I have longed after thy precepts: quicken me in thy righteousness.

Verses 33-40

The One Thousandth Psalm

O God, we thank Thee for everything.
   For the sea and its waves, blue, green and gray and
always wonderful;
For the beach and the breakers and the spray and the
   white foam on the rocks;
For the blue arch of heaven; for the clouds in the sky,
   white and gray and purple;
For the green of the grass; for the forests in their spring
   beauty; for the wheat and corn and rye and barley.
We thank Thee for all Thou hast made and that Thou hast
   called it good;
For all the glory and beauty and wonder of the world.
We thank Thee that Thou hast placed us in the world to
   subdue all things to Thy glory,
And to use all things for the good of Thy children.

Edward Everett Hale (1822-1909)

Prayer of Saint Patrick

May the wisdom of God instruct me, the
eye of God watch over me, the ear of God
hear me, the word of God give me sweet
talk, the hand of God defend me, the way
of God guide me.
   Christ be with me.
   Christ before me.

Christ in me.
Christ under me.
Christ over me.
Christ on my right hand.
Christ on my left hand.
Christ on this side.
Christ on that side.
Christ in the head of everyone to whom I speak.
Christ in the mouth of every person who speaks to me.
Christ in the eye of every person who looks upon me.
Christ in the ear of everyone who hears me today.
Amen.

Saint Patrick (389?-461)

Grant me, O Lord, to know what I ought to know,
to love what I ought to love,
to praise what delights Thee most,
to value what is precious in Thy sight,
to hate what is offensive to Thee.
Do not suffer me to judge according to the sight
of my eyes,
nor to pass sentence according to the hearing
of the ears of ignorant men;
but to discern with a true judgment
between things visible and spiritual,
and above all, always to inquire what is
the good pleasure of Thy will.

Thomas à Kempis (1380-1471)

Teach us, good Lord, to serve Thee as Thou deservest; to give and not to count the cost; to fight and not to heed the wounds; to toil and not to seek for rest; to labor and not to ask for any reward save that of knowing that we do Thy will.

Author Unknown

O Thou by whom we come to God,
The Life, the Truth, the Way—
The path of prayer Thyself hath trod,
Lord, teach us how to pray.

Author Unknown

O Lord, I know not what I ought to ask of thee; thou only knowest what I need; thou lovest me better than I know how to love myself. O Father! give to thy child that which he himself knows not how to ask. I dare not ask either for crosses or consolations; I simply present myself before thee, I open my heart to thee. Behold my needs which I know not myself; see and do according to thy mercy. Smite or heal, depress or raise me up; I adore all thy purposes without knowing them; I am silent; I offer myself in sacrifice; I yield myself to thee; I would have no other desire than to accomplish thy will. Teach me to pray. Pray thyself in me.

Francois De Salignac de la Mothe Fenelon

O Thou who art the Light of the minds that know Thee, the Life of the souls that love Thee and the Strength of the wills that serve Thee, help us so to know Thee that we may truly love Thee, so to love Thee that we may fully serve Thee, whom to serve is perfect freedom.

Author Unknown

O LORD, THOU knowest that which is best for us. Let this or that be done, as thou shalt please. Give what thou wilt, how much thou wilt, and when thou wilt.

Thomas à Kempis (1380-1471)

SEARCH ME, O God, and know my heart: try me, and know my thoughts: and see if there be any wicked way in me, and lead me in the way everlasting.

Psalm 139:23-24

GREAT SPIRIT, HELP me never to judge another until I have walked in his moccasins.

Sioux Indian Prayer

Prayers Of the Ages

O Heavenly Father, in Whom we live and move and have our being, we humbly pray Thee so to guide and govern us by Thy Holy Spirit, that in all the cares and occupations of our daily life we may never forget Thee, but remember that we are ever walking in Thy sight; for Thine own Name's sake. Amen.

An Ancient Collect (440)

THE PEACE OF God which passeth all understanding keep our hearts and minds in the knowledge and love of God, and of His Son Jesus Christ our Lord, and the blessing of God Almighty, the Father, the Son, and the Holy Ghost, be amongst you and remain with you always. Amen.

From the Book Of Common Prayer

O GOD, WHO hast prepared for them that love Thee such good things as pass man's understanding; pour into our hearts such love towards Thee, that we, loving Thee above all things, may obtain Thy promises, which exceed all that we can desire; through Jesus Christ our Lord. Amen.

From the Galasian Sacramentary

ALMIGHTY GOD, Who hast made all things for man, and man for Thy glory, sanctify our body and soul, our thoughts and our intentions, our words and actions, that whatsoever we shall think, or speak or do, may by us be designed to the glorification of Thy name...and let no pride or self-seeking, no impure motive or unworthy purpose, no little ends, and low imagination stain our spirit, and unhallow any of our words and actions. But let our body be a servant to our spirit, and both body and spirit servants of Jesus Christ. Amen.

Thomas á Kempis (1380-1471)

For God's Safe Keeping

May the strength of God pilot us. May the power of God preserve us. May the wisdom of God instruct us. May the hand of God protect us. May the way of God direct us. May the shield of God defend us.

May the host of God guard us against the snares of the Evil One and the temptations of the world.

May Christ be with us. Christ before us. Christ in us. Christ over us. May Thy salvation, O Lord, be always ours this day and for evermore. Amen.

Saint Patrick (389?-461)

O LORD, OUR GOD, under the shadow of Thy wings let us hope. Thou wilt support us, both when little, and even to gray hairs. When our strength is of Thee, it is strength; but, when our own, it is feebleness. We return unto Thee, O Lord, that from their weariness our souls may rise towards Thee; for with Thee is refreshment and true strength. Amen.

Saint Augustine (354-430)

MY SOUL, WAIT thou only upon God; for my expectation *is* from him. He only is my rock and my salvation: he *is* my defense; I shall not be moved. In God *is* my salvation and my glory: the rock of my strength, *and* my refuge, *is* in God.

Psalm 62:5-7

BECAUSE THOU HAST been my help, therefore in the shadow of thy wings will I rejoice.

Psalm 63:7

LORD JESUS, merciful and patient, grant us grace, I beseech Thee, ever to teach in a teachable spirit; learning along with those we teach, and learning from them whenever Thou so pleasest. Word of God, speak to us, speak by us, what Thou wilt. Wisdom of God, instruct us, instruct by us, if and whom Thou wilt. Eternal Truth, reveal Thyself to us, in whatever measure Thou wilt; that we and they may all be taught of God.

Christina Georgina Rossetti (1830-1894)

GIVE US, O Lord, steadfast hearts, which no unworthy thought can drag downwards; unconquered hearts, which no tribulation can wear out, upright hearts, which no unworthy purpose may tempt aside. Bestow upon us also, O Lord our God, understanding to know Thee, diligence to seek Thee, wisdom to find Thee, and a faithfulness that may finally embrace Thee.

Saint Thomas Aquinas (1224?-1274)

For This Universe

O God, we thank Thee for this universe, our great home; for its vastness and its riches, and for the manifoldness of the life which teems upon it and of which we are part. We praise Thee for the arching sky and the blessed winds, for the driving clouds and the constellations on high. We praise Thee for the salt sea and the running water, for the everlasting hills, for the trees, and for the grass under our feet.

We thank Thee for our senses by which we can see the splendor of the morning, and hear the jubilant songs of love, and smell the breath of the springtime.

Grant us, we pray Thee, a heart wide open to all this joy and beauty and save our souls from being so steeped in care or so darkened by passion that we pass heedless and unseeing when even the thornbush by the wayside is aflame with the glory of God.

Walter Rauschenbusch (1861-1918)

Prayers

O heavenly Father, protect and bless all things that have breath; guard them from all evil and let them sleep in peace.

Albert Schweitzer (1875-1965)

THANKS BE TO Thee, Lord Jesus Christ, for all the benefits which Thou hast won for us, for all the pains and insults which Thou hast borne for us. O most merciful Redeemer, Friend and Brother, may we know Thee more clearly, love Thee more dearly, and follow Thee more nearly, day by day.

Richard of Chichester (1197-1253)

LORD, I SHALL be verie busie this day. I may forget Thee but do not Thou forget me.

Sir Jacob Astley (1579-1652)

Dear Lord and Father Of Mankind

Dear Lord and Father of mankind,
   Forgive our foolish ways!
Reclothe us in our rightful mind,
In purer lives Thy service find,
In deeper reverence, praise.

Drop Thy still dews of quietness,
Till all our strivings cease;
Take from our souls the strain and stress,
And let our ordered lives confess
The beauty of Thy peace.

John Greenleaf Whittier (1807-1892)

O God, let me not turn coward before the difficulties of the day or prove recreant to its duties. Let me not lose faith in my fellowmen. Keep me sweet and sound of heart, in spite of ingratitude, treachery or meanness. Preserve me from minding little stings or giving them.

Author Unknown

These Are the Gifts I Ask

These are the gifts I ask
    Of Thee, Spirit serene:
Strength for the daily task,
    Courage to face the road,
Good cheer to help me bear the traveler's load,
And, for the hours of rest that come between,
An inward joy of all things heard and seen.

    These are the sins I fain
    Would have Thee take away:
    Malice and cold distain,
    Hot anger, sullen hate,
Scorn of the lowly, envy of the great,
And discontent that casts a shadow gray
On all the brightness of the common day.

Henry van Dyke (1852-1933)

If I Can

If I can stop one heart from breaking,
    I shall not live in vain;
If I can ease one life the aching,
    Or cool one pain,
Or help one fainting robin
Unto his nest again,
I shall not live in vain.

Emily Dickinson (1830-1886)

43

My Daily Prayer

If I can do some good today,
If I can serve along life's way,
If I can something helpful say,
Lord, show me how.

If I can right a human wrong,
If I can help to make one strong,
If I can cheer with smile or song,
Lord, show me how.

If I can aid one in distress,
If I can make a burden less,
If I can spread more happiness,
Lord, show me how.

Grenville Kleiser (1868-1953)

Just For Today

Lord, for tomorrow and its needs
I do not pray;
Keep me, my God, from stain of sin
Just for today.

Let me both diligently work,
And duly pray.
Let me be kind in word and deed,
Just for today.

Let me be slow to do my will,
Prompt to obey;
Help me to mortify my flesh
Just for today.

Let me no wrong or idle word
Unthinking say:
Set Thou a seal upon my lips
Just for today.

Let me in season, Lord, be grave,
Let me be gay,
Let me be faithful to Thy grace,
Just for today.

And if today my tide of life
Should ebb away,
Give me Thy sacraments divine,
Sweet Lord, today.

So for tomorrow and its needs
I do not pray,
But keep me, guide me, love me, Lord,
Just for today.

Samuel Wilberforce (1805-1873)

A Morning Prayer

Let me today do something that will take
  A little sadness from the world's vast store,
And may I be so favored as to make
  Of joy's too scanty sum a little more.

Let me not hurt, by any selfish deed
  Or thoughtless word, the heart of foe or friend.
Nor would I pass unseeing worthy need,
  Or sin by silence when I should defend.

However meager be my worldly wealth,
  Let me give something that shall aid my kind—
A word of courage, or a thought of health
  Dropped as I pass for troubled hearts to find.

Let me tonight look back across the span
  'Twixt dawn and dark, and to my conscience say—
Because of some good act to beast or man—
  "The world is better that I lived today."

Ella Wheeler Wilcox (1850-1919)

An Evening Prayer

If I have wounded any soul today,
  If I have caused one foot to go astray,
If I have walked in my own willful way—
  Good Lord, forgive.

If I have uttered idle words or vain,
If I have turned aside from want or pain
Lest I myself should suffer through the strain—
Good Lord, forgive.

If I have craved for joys that are not mine,
If I have let my wayward heart repine
Dwelling on things on earth, not things divine—
Good Lord, forgive.

If I have been perverse, or hard, or cold,
If I have longed for shelter in the fold
When Thou hast given me some part to hold—
Good Lord, forgive.

Forgive the sins I have confessed to Thee,
Forgive the secret sins I do not see;
That which I know not, Father, teach Thou me—
Help me to live.

C. Maude Battersby

Forgive

Forgive, O Lord, our severing ways,
The rival altars that we raise,
The wrangling tongues that mar thy praise!

Thy grace impart! In time to be
Shall one great temple rise to Thee
Thy Church our broad humanity.

White flowers of love its wall shall climb,
Soft bells of peace shall ring its chime,
Its days shall all be holy time.

A sweeter song shall then be heard,
Confessing, in a world's accord,
The inward Christ, the living Word.

That song shall swell from shore to shore.
One hope, one faith, one love restore
The seamless robe that Jesus wore.

John Greenleaf Whittier (1807-1892)

I Do Not Ask Thee, Lord

I do not ask Thee, Lord,
That all my life may be
An easy, smooth and pleasant path—
   'Twould not be good for me.
But, oh, I ask to-day
   That strength and grace be given
To keep me fighting all the way
   That leads to God and heaven!

I do not ask Thee, Lord,
    That tears may never flow,
Or that the world may always smile
    Upon me as I go.
From Thee fell drops of blood,
    A thorn-crown pressed Thy Brow,
Thy suffering brought Thee victory then,
    And Thou canst help me now.

And what if strength should fail,
    And heart more deeply bleed?
Or what if dark and lonely days
    Draw forth the cry of need?
That cry will bring Thee down,
    My needy soul to fill,
And Thou wilt teach my yearning heart
    To know and do Thy will.

Author Unknown

Daily Creed

L et me be a little kinder,
  Let me be a little blinder
To the faults of those about me,
Let me praise a little more.

Let me be, when I am weary,
Just a little bit more cheery;
Let me serve a little better
The God we would adore.

Let me be a little meeker
With the brother who is weaker;
Let me strive a little harder
To be all that I should be.

Let me be more understanding,
And a little less demanding,
Let me be the sort of friend
That you have always been to me.

John Gray (1839-1915?)

A Child's Prayer

Father, lead me, day by day,
   Ever in Thine own sweet way;
Teach me to be pure and true,
Show me what I ought to do.

When I'm tempted to do wrong,
Make me stedfast, wise and strong;
And when all alone I stand,
Shield me with Thy mighty hand.

When my heart is full of glee,
Help me to remember Thee—
Happy most of all to know
That my Father loves me so.

May I do the good I know,
Be Thy loving child below.
Then at last go home to Thee,
Evermore Thy child to be.

Author Unknown

God Give Me Joy

God give me joy in the common things:
In the dawn that lures, the eve that sings.

In the new grass sparkling after rain,
In the late wind's wild and weird refrain;

In the springtime's spacious field of gold,
In the precious light by winter doled.

God give me joy in the love of friends,
In their dear home talk as summer ends;

In the songs of children, unrestrained;
In the sober wisdom age has gained.

God give me joy in the tasks that press,
In the memories that burn and bless;

In the thought that life has love to spend,
In the faith that God's at journey's end.

God give me hope for each day that springs,
God give me joy in the common things!

Thomas Curtis Clark

I f there be some weaker one,
  Give me strength to help him on;
If a blinder soul there be,
Let me guide him nearer Thee.
Make my mortal dreams come true
With the work I fain would do;
Clothe with life the weak intent,
Let me be the thing I meant;
Let me find in Thy employ
Peace that dearer is than joy;
Out of self to love be led
And to heaven acclimated,
Until all things sweet and good
Seem my natural habitude.

John Greenleaf Whittier (1807-1892)
From "Andrew Rykman's Prayer"

Dedication

Thou, whose unmeasured temple stands,
 Built over earth and sea,
Accept the walls that human hands
Have raised, O God, to Thee!

Lord, from Thine inmost glory send,
Within these courts to bide,
The peace that dwelleth without end
Serenely by Thy side!

May erring minds that worship here
Be taught the better way;
And they who mourn, and they who fear,
Be strengthened as they pray.

May faith grow firm, and love grow warm,
And pure devotion rise,
While round these hallowed walls the storm
Of earthborn passion dies.

William Cullen Bryant (1794-1878)

More Favorites

More Favorites

More Favorites

More Favorites

More Favorites

Part Two

Treasured Poems and Quotations

Look To This Day

L ook to this day!
For it is life, the very life of life.
In its brief course lie all the verities
  and realities of your existence:
The bliss of growth;
The glory of action;
The splendor of beauty;
For yesterday is already a dream, and
  tomorrow is only a vision;
But today, well lived, makes every yesterday
A dream of happiness, and every tomorrow a
  vision of hope.
Look well, therefore, to this day!

From the Sanskrit

To Begin the Day

A moment in the morning, ere the cares of day begin,
Ere the heart's wide door is open for the world to
  enter in;
Ah, then alone with Jesus, in the silence of the morn,
In heavenly, sweet communion let your duty day be born.
In the quietude that blesses with a prelude of repose,
Let your soul be soothed and softened, as the dew revives
  the rose.

A moment in the morning, take your Bible in your hand,
And catch a glimpse of glory from the peaceful promised
  land;
It will linger still before you when you seek the busy
mart,
And, like flowers of hope, will blossom into beauty in
your heart;
The precious words, like jewels, will glisten all the day,
With a rare, effulgent glory that will brighten all the way.

A moment in the morning—a moment, if no more—
Is better than an hour when the trying day is o'er.
'Tis the gentle dew from heaven, the manna for the day;
If you fail to gather early—alas! it melts away.
So, in the blush of morning take the offered hand of love,
And walk in heaven's pathway and the peacefulness
thereof.

Author Unknown

Today

Mend a quarrel.
Search out a forgotten friend.
Dismiss suspicion and replace it with trust.
Write a love letter.
Share some treasure.
Give a soft answer.
Encourage youth.
Manifest your loyalty in a word or deed.

Keep a promise.
Find the time.
Forego a grudge.
Forgive an enemy.
Listen.
Apologize if you were wrong.
Try to understand.
Flout envy.

Examine your demands on others.
Think first of someone else.
Appreciate, be kind, be gentle.
Laugh a little more.
Deserve confidence.
Take up arms against malice.
Decry complacency.
Express your gratitude.

Worship your God.
Gladden the heart of a child.
Take pleasure in the beauty and wonder of the earth.
Speak your love.
Speak it again.
Speak it still again.
Speak it still once again.

Author Unknown

The only preparation for the morrow is the right use of today. The stone in the hands of the builder must be put in its place and fitted to receive another. The morrow comes for naught, if today is not heeded. Neglect not the call that comes to thee this day, for such neglect is nothing else than boasting thyself of tomorrow.

G. Bowen

BOAST NOT THYSELF of tomorrow; for thou knowest not what a day may bring forth.

Proverbs 27:1

THE ACTS OF breathing which I performed yesterday will not keep me alive today; I must continue to breathe afresh every moment, or animal life ceases. In like manner yesterday's grace and spiritual strength must be renewed, and the Holy Spirit must continue to breathe on my soul from moment to moment in order to my enjoying the consolations, and to my working the works of God.

August Montague Toplady (1740-1778)

A New Start

I will start anew this morning with a higher, fairer creed;
I will cease to stand complaining of my ruthless neighbor's greed;
I will cease to sit repining while my duty's call is clear;

I will waste no moment whining, and my heart shall
      know no fear.
I will look sometimes about me for the things that merit
      praise;
I will search for hidden beauties that elude the grumbler's
      gaze.
I will try to find contentment in the paths that I must
      tread;
I will cease to have resentment when another moves
      ahead.
I will not be swayed by envy when my rival's strength is
      shown;
I will not deny his merit, but I'll strive to prove my own;
I will try to see the beauty spread before me, rain or
      shine;
I will cease to preach your duty, and be more concerned
      with mine.

Author Unknown

God has a purpose for each one of us, a work for
each one to do, a place for each one to fill, an influence for each one to exert, a likeness to his dear Son
for each one to manifest, and then, a place for each one to
fill in his holy temple.

Arthur C. A. Hall

FIND YOUR PURPOSE and fling your life out into it;
and the loftier your purpose is, the more sure you will be

to make the world richer with every enrichment of
yourself.

Phillips Brooks (1835-1893)

AND WHATSOEVER YE do, do *it* heartily, as to the
Lord, and not unto men.

Colossians 3:23

THEREFORE, MY BELOVED brethren, be ye stedfast,
unmoveable, always abounding in the work of the Lord,
forasmuch as ye know that your labour is not in vain in
the Lord.

1 Corinthians 15:58

D o all the good you can,
   By all the means you can,
In all the ways you can,
In all the places you can,
At all the times you can,
To all the people you can,
As long as ever you can.

John Wesley (1703-1791)

WE HAVE A CALL to do good, as often as we have the
power and occasion.

William Penn (1644-1718)

I AM ONLY ONE, but I *am* one. I can't do everything, but I *can* do something. And what I *can* do, that I ought to do. And what I *ought* to do, by the grace of God, I *shall* do.

Edward Everett Hale (1822-1909)

Greeting

I salute you. I am your friend and my love for you goes deep. There is nothing I can give you which you have not got; but there is much, very much, that, while I cannot give it, you can take. No heaven can come to us unless our hearts find rest in today. Take heaven! No peace lies in the future which is not hidden in this present little instant. Take Peace! The gloom of the world is but a shadow. Behind it, yet within our reach, is joy. There is radiance and glory in the darkness, could we but see, and to see we have only to look. I beseech you to look.

Life is so generous a giver, but we, judging its gifts by their covering, cast them away as ugly or heavy or hard. Remove the covering and you will find beneath it a living splendour, woven of love, by wisdom, with power. Welcome it, grasp it, and you touch the angel's hand that brings it to you. Everything we call a trial, a sorrow, or a duty, believe me, that angel's hand is there; the gift is there, and the wonder of an over-shadowing Presence.

Our joys too: be not content with them as joys. They, too, conceal diviner gifts. Life is so full of meaning and purpose, so full of beauty, beneath its covering, that you will find earth but cloaks your heaven. Courage then to claim it: that is all! But courage you have, and the knowledge that we are pilgrims together, wending through an unknown country, home. And so, at this time, I greet you. Not quite as the world sends greetings, but with profound esteem and with the prayer that for you, now and forever, the day breaks, and the shadows flee away.

From a letter written by
Fra Giovanni *1513* A.D.

This Day Is Mine
To Mar Or Make

This day is mine to mar or make,
God keep me strong and true;
Let me no erring by-path take,
No doubtful action do.

Grant me when the setting sun
This fleeting day shall end,
I may rejoice o'er something done,
Be richer by a friend.

Let all I meet along the way
Speak well of me to-night.
I would not have the humblest say
I'd hurt him by a slight.

Let there be something true and fine
When night slips down to tell
That I have lived this day of mine
Not selfishly, but well.

Author Unknown

Just For Today, Lord

I will live through the next twelve hours and not try to
tackle all of life's problems at once.

I will improve my mind. I will learn something useful. I
will learn something that requires effort, thought, and
concentration.

I will be agreeable.

I will look my best, speak in a well-modulated voice, be
courteous and considerate.

I will not find fault with friend, relative, or colleague.

I will not try to change or improve anyone but myself.

I will have a program. I might not follow it exactly, but I
will have it.

I will save myself from two enemies—hurry and
indecision.

I will do a good turn and keep it a secret. If anyone finds
out, it won't count.

I will do two things I don't want to do, just for the
   exercise. I will believe in myself. I will give my best
   to the world and feel confident that the world will
   give its best to me.

Author Unknown

If there is righteousness in the heart,
   there will be beauty in the character.
If there be beauty in the character,
   there will be harmony in the home.
If there is harmony in the home,
   there will be order in the nation.
When there is order in the nation,
   there will be peace in the world.

Author Unknown

HE IS HAPPIEST, be he king or peasant, who finds his
peace in his home.

Johann Wolfgang von Goethe (1749-1832)

EVERY HOUSE WHERE love abides and friendship is a
guest, is surely home, and home, sweet home; for there
the heart can rest.

Henry van Dyke (1852-1933)

WHERE YOUR PLEASURE is, there is your treasure.
Where your treasure is, there is your heart.
Where your heart is, there is your happiness.

Saint Augustine (354-430)

IF A MAN does not keep pace with his companions, perhaps it is because he hears a different drummer. Let him step to the music which he hears, however measured or far away.

Henry Thoreau (1817-1862)

THE JOURNEY OF a thousand miles begins with one step.

Lao-tse (6th Cent. B.C.)

STRIVE FOR THE approval of your companions but do not be too easily moved by ridicule. When you know what you ought to do, permit not the laughter of others to deter you.

Frederick Starr

A FREE MIND is a great thing no doubt, but loftiness of heart, belief in goodness, capacity for enthusiasm and devotion, the thirst after perfection and holiness, are greater things still.

Amiel (1821-1881)

DO WHAT THOU lovest; paint or sing or carve. Do what thou lovest, though the body starve! Who works for glory oft may miss the goal. Who works for money merely starves the soul; work for the work's sake, then, and, it may be, these other things'll be added unto thee.

Author Unknown

DO NOT PRAY for easy lives! Pray to be stronger men. Do not pray for tasks equal to your powers. Pray for powers equal to your tasks. Then the doing of your work shall be no miracle, but you shall be a miracle.

Phillips Brooks (1835-1893)

HAPPINESS IN THIS world, when it comes, comes incidentally. Make it the object of pursuit, and it leads us a wild-goose chase, and is never attained. Follow some other object, and very possibly we may find that we have caught happiness without dreaming of it.

Nathaniel Hawthorne (1804-1864)

A TASK WITHOUT a vision is drudgery; a vision without a task is a dream; a task with a vision is victory.

Author Unknown

What can I give Him,
Poor as I am?
If I were a shepherd
I would bring a lamb.
If I were a Wise Man
I would do my part—
Yet what can I give Him,
Give my heart.

Christina Georgina Rossetti (1830-1894)

LOVE IS THE greatest thing that God can give us: for Himself is Love; and it is the greatest thing we can give to God: for it will give ourselves, and carry with it all that is ours.

Jeremy Taylor (1613-1667)

THE GREATEST AND the best talent that God gives to any man or woman in this world is the talent of prayer. And the best usury that any man or woman brings back to God when He comes to reckon with them at the end of this world is a life of prayer.

Alexander Whyte

THESE BE OUR prayers—more strength, more light, more constancy, more progress.

Phillips Brooks (1835-1893)

LIFE IS MADE up, not of great sacrifices or duties, but of little things, in which smiles and kindnesses and small obligations, given habitually, are what win and preserve the heart and secure comfort.

Sir Humphry Davy (1778-1829)

OUR TODAYS AND yesterdays are the blocks with which we build.

Henry Wadsworth Longfellow (1807-1882)

IS IT SO SMALL a thing to have enjoyed the sun, to have lived light in the spring, to have loved, to have thought, to have done?

Arnold

THE TRUE TEST of a man's worth is not his theology but his life.

The Talmud

THE DAY IS always his who works in it with serenity and great aims.

Ralph Waldo Emerson (1803-1882)

My Pacesetter

11/13/98

The Lord is my pacesetter,
I shall not rush.
He makes me to stop
for quiet intervals.
He provides me with images of stillness
which restore my serenity.
He leads me in ways of efficiency
through calmness of mind,
and His guidance
is peace.
Even though I have a great many things
to accomplish each day,
I will not fret
for His presence is here.
His timelessness,
His all-importance
will keep me in balance.
He prepares refreshment

in the midst of my activity
by anointing my mind
with His oil of tranquility.
My cup of joyous energy overflows.
Surely harmony and effectiveness
shall be the fruit of my hours,
And I shall walk
in the pace of the Lord
and dwell in His house
forever.

Author Unknown

A Time For Every Thing

To every *thing there is* a season, and a time to every purpose under the heaven:

A time to be born, and a time to die; a time to plant, and a time to pluck up *that which is* planted;

A time to kill, and a time to heal; a time to break down, and a time to build up;

A time to weep, and a time to laugh; a time to mourn, and a time to dance;

A time to cast away stones, and a time to gather stones together; a time to embrace, and a time to refrain from embracing;

A time to get, and a time to lose; a time to keep, and a time to cast away;

A time to rend, and a time to sew; a time to keep silence, and a time to speak;

A time to love, and a time to hate; a time of war, and a time of peace.

Ecclesiastes 3:1-8

What is time?
The shadow on the dial,
the striking of the clock,
the running of the sand,
day and night,
summer and winter,
months, years, centuries?
These are but arbitrary and outward signs,
the measure of time,
not time itself.
Time is the life of the soul.
If not this, then tell me, what is time?

Author Unknown

BUT, BELOVED, BE not ignorant of this one thing, that one day *is* with the Lord as a thousand years, and a thousand years as one day.

2 Peter 3:8

WAIT ON THE LORD: be of good courage, and he shall strengthen thine heart: wait, I say, on the LORD.

Psalm 27:14

FOR WE THROUGH the Spirit wait for the hope of righteousness by faith.

Galations 5:5

Time Is

Too Slow for those who Wait,
Too Swift for those who Fear,
Too Long for those who Grieve,
Too Short for those who Rejoice
But for those who Love,
Time is Eternity.

Henry van Dyke (1852-1933)

Hope is like a harebell trembling from its birth,
Love is like a rose the joy of all the earth,
Faith is like a lily lifted high and white,
Love is like a lovely rose the world's delight.

Harebells and sweet lilies show a thornless growth,
But the rose with all its thorns excels them both.

Christina Georgina Rossetti (1830-1894)

Time

Take time to pray...it helps to bring God near and washes the dust of earth from your eyes.
Take time for friends...it is the source of happiness.
Take time for work...it is the price of success.
Take time to think...it is the source of power.
Take time to read...it is the foundation of knowledge.
Take time to laugh...it is the singing that helps with life's loads.
Take time to love...it is the one sacrament of life.
Take time to dream...it hitches the soul to the stars.
Take time to play...it is the secret of youth.
Take time to worship...it is the highway to reverence.

Author Unknown

The Difference

I got up early one morning and rushed right into the day;
I had so much to accomplish that I didn't have time to
pray.

Problems just tumbled about me, and heavier came each
task;
"Why doesn't God help me?" I wondered. He answered,
"You didn't ask."

I wanted to see joy and beauty, but the day toiled on
gray and bleak;
I wondered why God didn't show me. He said, "But you
didn't seek."

I tried to come into God's presence; I used all my keys in
the lock.
God gently and lovingly chided, "My child, you didn't
knock."

I woke up early this morning, and paused before entering
the day;
I had so much to accomplish that I had to take time to
pray.

Author Unknown

Take Time

Take time to think; it is the source of power.
Take time to read; it is the foundation of wisdom.

Take time to play; it is the secret of staying young.
Take time to be quiet; it is the opportunity to seek God.

Take time to be aware; it is the opportunity to help
   others.
Take time to love and be loved; it is God's greatest gift.

Take time to laugh; it is the music of the soul.
Take time to be friendly; it is the road to happiness.

Take time to dream; it is what the future is made of.
Take time to pray; it is the greatest power on earth.

Author Unknown

Minutes Of Gold

Two or three minutes—two or three hours,
   What do they mean in this life of ours?
Not very much if but counted as time,
But minutes of gold and hours sublime,
If only we'll use them once in a while
To make someone happy—make someone smile.
A minute may dry a little lad's tears,

An hour sweep aside trouble of years.
Minutes of my time may bring to an end
Hopelessness somewhere, and bring me a friend.

Author Unknown

One Day At a Time

Finish every day and be done with it. You have done
what you could. Some blunders and absurdities no
doubt crept in; forget them as soon as you can. Tomorrow
is a new day; begin it well and serenely and with too
high a spirit to be cumbered with your old nonsense.
This day is all that is good and fair. It is too dear, with
its hopes and invitations, to waste a moment on
yesterdays.

Ralph Waldo Emerson (1803-1882)

Whoso Draws Nigh To God

Whoso draws nigh to God one step
through doubtings dim,
God will advance a mile
in blazing light to him.

Author Unknown

Faith

Nothing before, nothing behind;
The steps of faith
Fall on the seeming void, and find
The rock beneath.

John Greenleaf Whittier (1807-1892)

We Live By Faith

We live by faith; but faith is not the slave
Of text and legend. Reason's voice and God's;
Nature's and Duty's, never are at odds.
What asks our Father of His children, save
Justice, mercy and humility,
A reasonable service of good deeds,
Pure living, tenderness to human needs,
Reverence and trust, and prayer for light to see
The Master's footprints in our daily ways.

John Greenleaf Whittier (1807-1892)

Hope

S oft as the voice, as the voice of a
Zephyr, breathing unheard,
Hope gently whispers, through the shadows,
   Her comforting word:
Wait till the darkness is over,
   Wait till the tempest is done,
Hope for the sunshine, hope for the morrow,
   After the storm has gone.

Author Unknown

H ope is wishing for a thing to come true;
faith is believing that it will come true.

Norman Vincent Peale (1898-   )

WHERE THERE IS faith, there is love;
Where there is love, there is peace;
Where there is peace, there is God;
And where there is God, there is no need.

Leo Tolstoy (1828-1910)

Faith, Hope, and Love

FAITH sees beyond the grave,
A home of rest;
And whispers in the gloom,
"God's will is best."

HOPE, like a shining star,
Brightens life's way;
Gives courage to the faint,
From day to day.

LOVE, greatest gift of all,
Calms ev'ry fear;
Makes all our burdens light,
Brings Heaven near.

Author Unknown

And now abideth faith, hope, charity, these three; but the greatest of these *is* charity.

1 Corinthians 13:13

A Prayer For Faith

I pray for faith, I long to trust;
I listen with my heart, and hear

A Voice without a sound: "Be just,
   Be true, be merciful, revere
   The Word within thee; God is near!

"A light to sky and earth unknown
   Pales all their lights: a mightier force
Than theirs the powers of Nature own,
   And, to its goal as at its source,
   His Spirit moves the Universe.

"Believe and trust. Through stars and suns,
   Through life and death, through soul and sense,
His wise, paternal purpose runs;
   The darkness of His providence
   Is star-lit with benign intents."

O joy supreme! I know the Voice,
   Like none beside on earth or sea;
Yea, more, O soul of mine, rejoice,
   By all that He requires of me,
   I know what God himself must be....
I fear no more. The clouded face
   O Nature smiles; through all her things
Of time and space and sense I trace
   The moving of the Spirit's wings,
   And hear the song of hope she sings.

John Greenleaf Whittier (1807-1892)

To Make This Life Worthwhile

May every soul that touches mine,
Be it the slightest contact,
Get therefrom some good;
Some little grace; one kindly thought;
One aspiration yet unfelt;
One bit of courage
For the darkening sky;
One gleam of faith
To brave the thickening ills of life;
One glimpse of brighter skies
Beyond the gathering mists,
To make this life worthwhile.

George Eliot (1819-1880)

God's Will For Us

Just to be tender, just to be true;
Just to be glad the whole day through;
Just to be merciful, just to be mild;
Just to be trustful as a child;
Just to be gentle and kind and sweet;
Just to be helpful with willing feet;
Just to be cheery when things go wrong;
Just to drive sadness away with a song;
Whether the hour is dark or bright;
Just to be loyal to God and right;

Just to believe that God knows best;
Just in His promise ever to rest;
Just to let love be our daily key:
This is God's will, for you and me.

Author Unknown

God's Will Is Best

Thy Will is best for me,
    Whate'er it bringeth me;
Of loss or gain, of joy or pain,
Thy Will is best for me.

Author Unknown

We should give God the same place in our hearts
that he holds in the universe.

Author Unknown

KEEP US LORD so awake in the duties of our callings
that we may sleep in peace and awake in thy glory.

John Donne (1572-1631)

OUR GREATEST DANGER in life is in permitting the
urgent things to crowd out the important.

Charles E. Hummel

NO MAN IS born into the world whose work is not born with him. There is always work, and tools to work withal, for those who will.

James Russell Lowell (1819-1891)

WHATEVER GOD GIVES you to do, do it as well as you can. This is the best possible preparation for what He may want you to do next.

George Macdonald (1824-1905)

HAVE THY TOOLS ready; God will find thee work.

Charles Kingsley (1819-1875)

DO LITTLE THINGS as if they were great, because of the majesty of the Lord Jesus Christ, who dwells in thee; and do great things as if they were little and easy, because of His omnipotence.

Blaise Pascal (1623-1662)

IT IS NEITHER talent, nor power, nor gifts that do the work of God, but it is that which lies within the power of the humblest; it is the simple, earnest life hid with Christ in God.

F. W. Robertson (1816-1853)

GOD HOLDS US responsible not for what we have, but for what we might have; not for what we are, but for what we might be.

Mark Guy Pearse (1842-1930)

EVERYBODY THINKS OF changing humanity and no-body thinks of changing himself.

Leo Tolstoy (1828-1910)

LORD, WHERE WE are wrong, make us willing to change, and where we are right, make us easy to live with.

Peter Marshall (1902-1949)

Four Things To Do

Four things a man must learn to do
If he would keep his record true:
To think, without confusion, clearly;
To love his fellow-man sincerely;
To act from honest motives purely;
To trust in God and Heaven securely.

Henry van Dyke (1852-1933)

He teaches patience—by being gentle and under-standing over and over.
He teaches honesty—by keeping his promises to his family
even when it costs.
He teaches courage—by living unafraid, with faith,
in all circumstances.

He teaches justice—by being fair and dealing equally
   with everyone.
Every father can teach Christian principles.
He teaches kindness—by being thoughtful and gracious
   even at home.

Author Unknown

If I have faltered more or less
In my great task of happiness;
If I have moved among my race
And shown no shining morning face;
If beams from happy human eyes
Have moved me not; if morning skies,
Books, and my food, and summer rain
Knocked on my sullen heart in vain;
Lord, thy most pointed pleasure take
And stab my spirit broad awake.

Robert Louis Stevenson (1850-1894)

Very little is needed to make a happy life. It is all
within yourself, in your way of thinking.

Marcus Aurelius (121-180 A.D.)

AND BE RENEWED in the spirit of your mind.

Ephesians 4:23

HAPPY *IS* THE man *that* findeth wisdom, and the man *that* getteth understanding.

Proverbs 3:13

Understanding

Not more of light I ask, O God,
But eyes to see what is.
Not sweeter songs, but ears to hear
The present melodies.
Not more of strength, but how to use
The power that I possess.
Not more of love, but skill to turn
A frown to a caress.
Not more of joy, but how to feel
Its kindly presence near,
To give to others all I have
Of courage and of cheer.
No other gifts, dear God, I ask,
But only sense to see
How best these precious gifts to use
Thou hast bestowed on me.

Author Unknown

E verywhere I find the signature, the autograph of
God, and he will never deny his own handwriting.
God hath set his tabernacle in the dewdrop as surely as
in the sun. No man can any more create the smallest
flower than he could create the greatest world.

Joseph Parker (1830-1902)

IN ALL RANKS of life the human heart yearns for the
beautiful; and the beautiful things that God makes are
His gift to all alike.

Harriet Beecher Stowe (1811-1896)

THE BEAUTY OF the sunbeam lies partly in the fact
that God does not keep it; he gives it away to us all.

David Swing

THE PLEASANTEST THINGS in the world are pleasant thoughts: and the great art of life is to have as many
of them as possible.

Montaigne (1533-1592)

NATURE IS THE art of God.

Dante (1265-1321)

ART IS THE gift of God, and must be used unto His
glory. That in art is highest which aims at this.

Michelangelo (1475-1564)

ONE OUGHT EVERY day at least to hear a little song, read a good poem, see a fine picture, and, if it were possible, to speak a few reasonable words.

Johann Wolfgang von Goethe (1749-1832)

I SHALL PASS through this world but once. If, therefore, there be any kindness I can show, or any good thing I can do, let me do it now; let me not defer it or neglect it, for I shall not pass this way again.

De Grellet

LET US MAKE haste to live, since every day to a wise man is a new life.

Seneca

RULE YOURSELF. Love your neighbor. Do the duty that lies nearest you.

Alcott

THAT BEST PORTION of a good man's life: His little, nameless, unremembered acts of kindness and of love.

William Wordsworth (1770-1850)

DON'T WASTE LIFE in doubts and fears; spend yourself on the work before you, well assured that the right performance of this hour's duties will be the best preparation for the hours or ages that follow it.

Ralph Waldo Emerson (1803-1882)

QUIET MINDS CANNOT be perplexed or frightened, but go on in fortune or misfortune at their own private pace, like a clock in a thunderstorm.

Robert Louis Stevenson (1850-1894)

HAVE I NOT commanded thee? Be strong and of a good courage; be not afraid, neither be thou dismayed: for the LORD thy God *is* with thee whithersoever thou goest.

Joshua 1:9

FOR GOD HATH not given us the spirit of fear; but of power, and of love, and of a sound mind.

Timothy 1:7

IF ANY MAN seeks for greatness, let him forget greatness and ask for truth, and he will find both.

Horace Mann (1796-1859)

IT MATTERS NOT what you are thought to be, but what you are.

Syrus (1st Century B.C.)

LET US, THEN, be what we are, and speak what we think, and in all things keep ourselves loyal to truth and the sacred profession of friendship.

Henry Wadsworth Longfellow (1807-1882)

NO MAN CAN afford to invest his being in anything lower than faith, hope, love—these three, the greatest of which is love.

Henry Ward Beecher (1813-1887)

DOST THOU LOVE life? Then do not squander time, for that is the stuff life is made of.

Benjamin Franklin (1706-1790)

THE ONLY RELIGION that will do anything toward enriching your life is the religion which inspires you to do something toward enriching the life of others.

Author Unknown

AND LET EACH try, by great thoughts and good deeds to show the most of Heaven he hath in him.

Bailey

Good name in man and woman, dear my lord,
Is the immediate jewel of their souls:
Who steals my purse steals trash; 'tis something, nothing;
'Twas mine, 'tis his, and has been slave to thousands;
But he that filches from me my good name
Robs me of that which not enriches him,
And makes me poor indeed.

William Shakespeare (1564-1616)
From "Othello"

ONE OF THE purest and most enduring of human pleasures is to be found in the possession of a good name
among one's neighbors and acquaintances.

Charles William Eliot (1834-1926)

A GOOD NAME is better than precious ointment.

Ecclesiastes 7:1

A GOOD NAME *is* rather to be chosen than great
riches, *and* loving favor rather than silver and gold.

Proverbs 22:1

WORDS ARE INSTRUMENTS of music: an ignorant
man uses them for jargon; but when a master touches
them they have unexpected life and soul. Some words
sound out like drums; some breathe memories sweet as
flutes; some call like a clarionet; some show a charge like
trumpets; some are sweet as children's talk; others rich as
a mother's answering back.

Author Unknown

LIFE IS MUSIC if one be rightly in tune and in time.

Author Unknown

LIFE IS LIKE music; it must be composed by ear, feel-
ing, and instinct, not by rule.

Samuel Butler (1612-1680)

BEAUTY OF STYLE and harmony and grace and good rhythm depend on simplicity.

Plato (428-347? B.C.)

A Smile Costs Nothing

A smile costs nothing, but gives much.
It enriches those who receive, without making poorer those who give.

It takes but a moment, but the memory of it sometimes lasts forever.

None is so rich or mighty that he can get along without it, and none is so poor but that he can be made rich by it.

A smile creates happiness in the home, fosters good will in business, and is the countersign of friendship.

It brings rest to the weary, cheer to the discouraged, sunshine to the sad, and it is nature's best antidote for trouble.

Yet it cannot be bought, begged, borrowed, or stolen, for it is something that is of no value to anyone until it is given away.

Some people are too tired to give you a smile. Give them one of yours, as none needs a smile so much as he who has no more to give.

Author Unknown

The Tide

There is a tide in the affairs of men
  Which taken at the flood, leads on to fortune;
Omitted, all the voyage of their life,
Is bound in shallows and in miseries.

William Shakespeare (1564-1616)

No Return

Three things return not, even for prayers and tears—
  The arrow which the archer shoots at will;
The spoken word, keen-edged and sharp to sting;
The opportunity left unimproved.
If thou would'st speak a word of loving cheer,
Oh, speak it now. This moment is thine own.

Author Unknown

There are three marks of a superior man: being virtu-
  ous, he is free from anxiety; being wise, he is free
from perplexity; being brave, he is free from fear.

Confucius (551-479 B.C.)

The Unknown Future

Life is a book in volumes three—
The past, the present, and the yet-to-be.
The past is written and laid away,
The present we're writing every day,
And the last and best of volumes three
Is locked from sight—God keeps the key.

Author Unknown

Look not mournfully into the Past. It comes not back again. Wisely improve the Present. It is thine. Go forth to meet the shadowy Future, without fear, and with a manly heart.

Henry Wadsworth Longfellow (1807-1882)

ONLY ONE THING is necessary; to possess God.

Amiel (1821-1881)

SURELY GOD ENDURES forever.

James Russell Lowell (1819-1891)

Splendid Gift

L ive your life while you have it. Life is a splendid gift. There is nothing small in it. For the greatest things grow by God's Law out of the smallest. But to live your life you must discipline it. You must not fritter it away in "fair purpose, erring act, inconstant will" but make your thoughts, your acts, all work to the same end and that end, not self but God. That is what we call character.

Florence Nightingale (1820-1910)

For Whom the Bell Tolls

N o man is an island entire of itself. Every man is a piece of the continent, a part of the main. If a clod be washed away by the sea, Europe is the less, as well as if a promontory were, as well as if a manor of thy friends or of thine own were. Any man's death diminishes me, because I am involved in mankind. Therefore never send to know for whom the bell tolls. It tolls for thee.

John Donne (1572-1631)

Windows For My Soul

I will hew great windows for my soul,
Channels of splendor, portals of release;
Out of earth's prison walls will I hew them,
That my thundering soul may push through them;
Through the strata of human strife and passion
I will tunnel a way, I will carve and fashion
With the might of my soul's intensity
Windows fronting on immensity,
Towering out of time.
I will breathe the air of another clime
That my spirit's pain may cease.
That the being of me may have room to grow,
That my eyes may meet God's eyes and know;
I will hew great windows, wonderful windows,
Measureless windows for my soul.

Author Unknown

The Zest of Life

Let me but live my life from year to year,
With forward face and unreluctant soul.
Not hastening to, nor turning from the goal;
Not mourning for the things that disappear
In the dim past, nor holding back in fear
From what the future veils; but with a whole
And happy heart, that pays its toll

To youth and age, and travels on with cheer.
So let the way wind up the hill or down,
   Through rough or smooth, the journey will be joy;
   Still seeking what I sought but when a boy,
New friendship, high adventure, and a crown,
   I shall grow old, but never lose life's zest,
   Because the road's last turn will be the best.

Henry van Dyke (1852-1933)

All Thro' the Year

The world's a weary place,
For him who tries to face
   His tasks alone.
But he who looks above,
Will see the God of love
Is always swift to move
   Among His own.
And so I wish for thee
The vision clear to see,
   A presence near;
That every hour of night
And all the days of light,
May with God's love shine bright
   All thro' the year.

Author Unknown

G od reveals Himself unfailingly to the thoughtful
   seeker.

Honore de Balzac (1799-1850)

WHAT WE MUST do, let us love to do. Never lose an
opportunity to see anything beautiful. Beauty is God's
handwriting.

Charles Kingsley (1819-1875)

A THING OF beauty is a joy forever:
Its loveliness increases; it will never
Pass into nothingness; but still will keep
A bower quiet for us, and a sleep
Full of sweet dreams, and health, and quiet breathing.

John Keats (1795-1821)

THERE IS BEAUTY in the forest
   When the trees are green and fair,
There is beauty in the meadow
   When wild flowers scent the air.
There is beauty in the sunlight
   And the soft blue beams above.
Oh, the world is full of beauty
   When the heart is full of love.

Author Unknown

Footprints

One night a man had a dream. He dreamed he was walking along the beach with the Lord. Across the sky flashed scenes from his life. For each scene, he noticed two sets of footprints in the sand: one belonging to him, and the other to the Lord.

When the last scene of his life flashed before him, he looked back at the footprints in the sand. He noticed that many times along the path of his life there was only one set of footprints. He also noticed that it happened at the very lowest and saddest times in his life.

This really bothered him and he questioned the Lord about it. "Lord, You said that once I decided to follow You, You'd walk with me all the way. But I have noticed that during the most troublesome times in my life, there is only one set of footprints. I don't understand why when I needed You most You would leave me."

The Lord replied, "My son, My precious child, I love you and would never leave you. During your times of trial and suffering, when you see only one set of footprints, it was then that I carried you."

Author Unknown

E re thou sleepest, gently lay
  Every troubled thought away;
Put off worry and distress
As thou puttest off thy dress;
Drop thy burden and thy care
In the quiet arms of prayer.
Lord thou knowest how I live,
All I've done amiss forgive;
All of good I've tried to do
Strengthen, bless and carry through;
All I love in safety keep
While in Thee I fall asleep.

Henry van Dyke (1852-1933)

LET NOTHING DISTURB thee,
Nothing affright thee;
All things are passing:
God never changeth;
Patient endurance
Attaineth to all things;
Who God possesseth
In nothing is wanting;
Alone God sufficeth.

Saint Teresa of Avila (1515-1582)

I ASKED GOD for strength,
   that I might achieve,
I was made weak, that I
   might learn humbly to obey.

I asked for health, that I might
  do greater things,
I was given infirmity, that I might
  do better things.
I asked for riches, that I might be happy,
I was given poverty, that I might be wise.
I asked for power, that I might
  have the praise of men,
I was given weakness, that I
  might feel the need of God.
I asked for all things, that I
  might enjoy life,
I was given life, that I might
  enjoy all things.
I got nothing that I asked for—
  but everything I had hoped for.
Almost despite myself, my
  unspoken prayers were answered.
I am, among all men,
  most richly blessed.

Anonymous Confederate Soldier

What I Owe

If I have strength, I owe the service of the strong;
If melody I have, I owe the world a song.
If I can stand when all around my post are falling,
If I can run with speed when needy hearts are calling,
And if my torch can light the dark of any night,
Then, I must pay the debt I owe with living light.

For any gift God gives to me I cannot pay;
Gifts are most mine when I most give them all away,
God's gifts are like His flowers, which show their
   right to stay
By giving all their bloom and fragrance away;
Riches are not in gold or land, estates or marts,
The only wealth worth having is found in human hearts.

Author Unknown

May You Have

Enough happiness to keep you sweet,
Enough trials to keep you strong,
Enough sorrow to keep you human,
Enough hope to keep you happy;
Enough failure to keep you humble,
Enough success to keep you eager,
Enough friends to give you comfort,
Enough wealth to meet your needs;
Enough enthusiasm to look forward,
Enough faith to banish depression,
Enough determination to make each day
   better than yesterday.

Author Unknown

Nine Keys To Contentment

Health enough to make work a pleasure.
Wealth enough to support your needs.
Strength enough to battle with difficulties and
  overcome them.
Grace enough to confess your sins and forsake them.
Patience enough to toil until some good is accomplished.
Charity enough to see some good in your neighbors.
Love enough to move you to be useful and helpful to
  others.
Faith enough to make real things of God.
Hope enough to remove all anxious fears concerning the
  future.

Johann Wolfgang von Goethe (1749-1832)

Attainment

Use all your hidden forces. Do not miss
  The purpose of this life, and do not wait
For circumstance to mold or change your fate.
In your own self lies destiny. Let this
Vast truth cast out all fear, all prejudice,
All hesitation. Know that you are great,
Great with divinity. So dominate
Environment, and enter into bliss.
Love largely and hate nothing. Hold no aim
That does not chord with universal good.

Hear what the voices of the silence say,
All joys are yours if you put forth your claim,
Once let the spiritual laws be understood,
Material things must answer and obey.

Ella Wheeler Wilcox (1850-1919)

Light Shining Out Of Darkness

God moves in a mysterious way
His wonders to perform;
He plants His footsteps in the sea,
And rides upon the storm.

Deep in unfathomable mines
Of never-failing skill
He treasures up His bright designs,
And works His sovereign will.

Ye fearful saints, fresh courage take;
The clouds ye so much dread
Are big with mercy, and shall break
In blessings on your head.

Judge not the Lord by feeble sense,
But trust Him for His grace;
Behind a frowning providence

He hides a smiling face.

His purposes will ripen fast,
Unfolding every hour;
The bud may have a bitter taste,
But sweet will be the flower.

Blind unbelief is sure to err,
And scan His work in vain;
God is His own interpreter,
And He will make it plain.

William Cowper (1731-1800)

He Leadeth Me

In pastures green? Not always; sometimes He
Who knoweth best, in kindness leadeth me
In weary ways, where heavy shadows be.

Out of the sunshine warm and soft and bright,
Out of the sunshine into darkest night;
I oft would faint with sorrow and affright.

Only for this—I know He holds my hand,
So whether in the green or desert land.
I trust, although I may not understand.

And by still waters? No, not always so;
Oft times the heavy tempests round me blow,

And o'er my soul the waves and billows go.

But when the storms beat loudest, and I cry
Aloud for help, the Master standeth by,
And whispers to my soul, "Lo, it is I."

Above the tempest wild I hear Him say,
"Beyond this darkness lies the perfect day,
In every path of thine I lead the way."

So, whether on the hill-tops high and fair
I dwell, or in the sunless valleys where
The shadows lie—what matter? He is there.

And more than this; where'er the pathway lead
He gives to me no helpless, broken reed,
But His own hand, sufficient for my need.

So where He leads me I can safely go;
And in the blest hereafter I shall know
Why in His wisdom He hath led me so.

H. H. Barry

I Am Not Bound To Win

I am not bound to win,
But I am bound to be true.
I am not bound to succeed,
But I am bound to live up to what light I have.
I must stand with anybody that stands right;
Stand with him while he is right,
And part with him when he goes wrong.

Abraham Lincoln (1809-1865)

The Way

Who seeks for heaven alone to save his soul
May keep the path, but will not reach the goal;
While he who walks in love may wander far,
Yet God will bring him where the blessed are.

Henry van Dyke (1852-1933)

Don't Quit

When things go wrong as they sometimes will,
When the road you're trudging seems all uphill,
When the funds are low, and the debts are high,
And you want to smile, but you have to sigh,
When care is pressing you down a bit—
Rest if you must, but don't you quit.

Success is failure turned inside out,
    The silver tint of the clouds of doubt,
And you never can tell how close you are,
    It may be near when it seems afar.
So, stick to the fight when you're hardest hit—
    It's when things go wrong that you mustn't quit.

Author Unknown

A Winner's Creed

If you think you are beaten, you are;
If you think you dare not, you don't;
If you'd like to win, but think you can't,
    It's almost a cinch you won't.

If you think you'll lose, you're lost,
    For out in the world we find
Success begins with a person's faith;
    It's all in the state of mind.

Life's battles don't always go
    To the stronger or faster hand;
They go to the one who trusts in God
    And always thinks "I can."

Author Unknown

I can do all things through Christ which strengtheneth me.

Philippans 4:13

Try the Uplook

When the outlook is dark, try the uplook.
　　These words hold a message of cheer;
Be glad while repeating them over,
　　And smile when the shadows appear.
Above and beyond stands the Master:
　　He sees what we do for His sake.
He never will fail nor forsake us;
　　He knoweth the way that we take.

When the outlook is dark, try the uplook,
　　The outlook of faith and good cheer;
The love of the Father surrounds us,
　　He knows when the shadows are near.
Be brave, then, and keep the eyes lifted,
　　And smile on the dreariest day.
His smile will glow in the darkness;
　　His light will illumine the way.

Author Unknown

Give Thanks

For all that God, in mercy, sends;
  For health and children, home and friends;
For comfort in the time of need,
For every kindly word and deed,
For happy thoughts and holy talk,
For guidance in our daily walk—
  For everything give thanks!

For beauty in this world of ours,
For verdant grass and lovely flowers,
For song of birds, for hum of bees,
For the refreshing summer breeze,
For hill and plain, for stream and wood,
For the great ocean's mighty flood—
  For everything give thanks!

For the sweet sleep which comes with night,
For the returning morning's light,
For the bright sun that shines on high,
For the stars glittering in the sky—
For these, and everything we see,
O Lord! our hearts we lift to Thee—
  For everything give thanks!

Author Unknown

Rest

Are you very weary? Rest a little bit.
In some quiet corner, fold your hands
and sit.
Do not let the trials that have grieved
you all the day
Haunt this quiet corner; drive them
all away!
Let your heart grow empty of every
thought unkind
That peace may hover round you, and
joy may fill your mind.
Count up all your blessings, I'm sure
they are not few,
That the dear Lord daily just bestows
on you.
Soon you'll feel so rested, glad you
stopped a bit,
In this quiet corner, to fold your hands
and sit.

Author Unknown

The World Is Mine

Today, upon a bus, I saw a lovely girl with
golden hair.
I envied her, she seemed so gay; I wished I
were as fair.

When suddenly she rose to leave, I saw her
  hobble down the aisle;
She had one leg, and wore a crutch, and as
  she passed—a smile.
O God, forgive me when I whine;
  I have two legs. The world is mine.

And when I stopped to buy some sweets, the
  lad who sold them had such charm.
I talked with him—he seemed so glad—if we
  are late 'twould do no harm.
And as I left he said to me, "I thank you.
  You have been so kind.
It's nice to talk with folks like you. You
  see," he said, "I'm blind."
O God, forgive me when I whine.
  I have two eyes. The world is mine.

Later, walking down the street, I saw a child
  with eyes of blue.
He stood and watched the others play;
  seemed he knew not what to do.
I stopped a moment, then I said: "Why
  don't you join the others, Dear?"
He looked ahead without a word, and then
  I knew—He could not hear.
O God, forgive me when I whine.
I have two ears. The world is mine.

With legs to take me where I'd go,
With eyes to see the sunset's glow,
With ears to hear what I would know.
O God, forgive me when I whine.
I'm blessed indeed. The world is mine.

Author Unknown

A Child

If a child lives with criticism he learns
to condemn.
If a child lives with hostility he learns
to fight.
If a child lives with fear he learns to be
apprehensive.
If a child lives with pity he learns to feel
sorry for himself.
If a child lives with jealousy he learns to
hate.
If a child lives with encouragement he learns
to be confident.
If a child lives with praise he learns to
be appreciative.
If a child lives with approval he learns to
like himself.
If a child lives with recognition he learns to
have a goal.
If a child lives with fairness he learns
justice.

If a child lives with friendliness he learns
   that the world is a nice place in which to
   live.

Author Unknown

Train up a child in the way he should go: and when he is old, he will not depart from it.

Proverbs 22:6

EVEN A CHILD is known by his doings, whether his work *be* pure, and whether *it be* right.

Proverbs 20:11

CHILDREN, OBEY *YOUR* parents in all things: for this is well pleasing unto the Lord. Fathers, provoke not your children *to anger*, lest they be discouraged.

Colossians 3:20-21

JESUS SAID, "SUFFER little children, and forbid them not, to come unto me: for of such is the kingdom of heaven."

Matthew 19:14

THE SPIRIT ITSELF beareth witness with our spirit, that we are the children of God: And if children, then heirs; heirs of God, and joint-heirs with Christ; if so be that we suffer with him, that we may be also glorified together.

Romans 8:16-17

One Solitary Life

He was born in an obscure village. He worked in a carpenter shop until He was 30. He then became an itinerant preacher.

He never held an office. He never had a family or owned a house. He didn't go to college. He had no credentials but Himself.

He was only 33 when the public turned against Him. His friends ran away. He was turned over to His enemies and went through the mockery of a trial. He was nailed to a cross between two thieves. While He was dying, His executioners gambled for His clothing, the only property He had on earth. He was laid in a borrowed grave.

Nineteen centuries have come and gone, and today He is the central figure of the human race. All the armies that ever marched, all the navies that ever sailed, all the parliaments that ever sat, and all the kings that ever reigned, have not affected the life of man on this earth as much at that One Solitary Life.

Author Unknown

What Christ Is To Us

The Shield from every dart;
The Balm for every smart;
The Sharer of each load;
Companion on the road.

The Door into the fold;
The Anchor that will hold;
The Shepherd of the sheep;
The Guardian of my sleep.

The Friend with Whom I talk;
The Way by which I walk;
The Light to show the way;
The Strength for every day.

The Source of my delight;
The Song to cheer the night;
The Thought that fills my mind;
The Best of All to find—is Jesus!

Author Unknown

To be in Christ is to live in His ideas, character, spirit, as the atmosphere of being. Men everywhere are living in the ideas and characters of others. He who lives in the spirit of Raphael becomes a painter; he who lives in the spirit of Milton becomes a poet; he who lives in the spirit of Bacon becomes a philosopher; he who lives in the spirit of Caesar becomes a warrior; he who lives in the spirit of Christ becomes a man.

Author Unknown

IT IS IN the Word that we receive and embrace him, and so where the Word of Christ dwells richly, there Christ dwells. If the Word be in us at home, then we abide in Christ, and he in us. The ground of our hope is Christ in the world, but the evidence of our hope is Christ in the heart.

Matthew Henry (1662-1714)

YE ARE THE light of the world. A city that is set on a hill cannot be hid. Neither do men light a candle, and put it under a bushel, but on a candlestick; and it giveth light unto all that are in the house. Let your light so shine before men, that they may see your good works, and glorify your Father which is in heaven.

Matthew 5:14-16

LAMPS DO NOT talk, but they do shine. A lighthouse sounds no drum, it beats no gong; and yet far over the waters its friendly spark is seen by the mariner. So let your actions shine out your religion. Let the main sermon of your life be illustrated by all your conduct.

Charles W. Spurgeon (1834-1892)

IN EVERY GREETING we give to another on the street, in every moment's conversation, in every letter we write, in every contact with other lives, there is a subtle influence that goes from us that often reaches further, and leaves a deeper impression that the things themselves that we are doing at the time. It is not so much what we *do* in this world as what we *are*, that tells in spiritual results and impressions.

J. R. Miller

FOR YOU, LORD, I would labor, I would live,
To You would offer every passing hour;
My self, my time, my yielded will I give,
A witness of Your love's constraining power.

Author Unknown

IN THE PAST the Lord has helped us,
Guiding, loving all the way;
Let us therefore trust His promise:
Grace sufficient for each day!

Author Unknown

WE CANNOT LIVE our lives alone,
For other lives we touch
Are either strengthened by our own
Or weakened just as much.

Author Unknown

NOTHING IS LOST that is done for the Lord,
Let it be ever so small;
The smile of the Savior approves of the deed,
As though it were greatest of all.

Author Unknown

THE LITTLE LAMPS of friendship
We light along the way
Go shining on far down the years
To brighten up our day.

Author Unknown

LOOK UPON YOUR brother's need,
Love demands the loving deed;
Tell him that you love him true,
Prove it by the deed you do.

Author Unknown

NOT IN HAVING or receiving,
But in giving, there is bliss;
He who has no other pleasure
Ever may rejoice in this.

Author Unknown

GIVE ME TO serve in humble sphere;
I ask not ought beside,
Content to fill a little place
If God be glorified.

Author Unknown

GIVE ME, SAVIOR, a purpose deep,
In joy or sorrow Your trust to keep;
And so through trouble, care, and strife,
To keep You first in my daily life.

Author Unknown

PRECIOUS SOULS ARE in our keeping,
God requires them at our hand;
Ask yourself, dear fellow Christian,
"Am I doing all I can?"

Author Unknown

I Met The Master

I had walked life's way with an easy tread,
Had followed where comforts and pleasures led.
Until one day in a quiet place
I met the Master face to face.

With station and rank and wealth for my goal,
Much thought for my body but none for my soul,
I had entered to win in life's mad race,
When I met the Master face to face.

I met Him and knew Him and blushed to see
That His eyes full of sorrow were fixed on me;
And I faltered and fell at His feet that day,
While my castles melted and vanished away.

Melted and vanished and in their place
Naught else did I see but the Master's face.
And I cried aloud, "Oh, make me meet
To follow the steps of Thy wounded feet."

My thought is now for the souls of men,
I have lost my life to find it again,
E'er since one day in a quiet place
I met the Master face to face.

Author Unknown

Heaven often seems distant and unknown, but if He who made the road thither is our guide, we need not fear to lose the way. We do not want to see far ahead—only far enough to discern Him and trace His footsteps.... They who follow Christ, even through darkness, will surely reach the Father.

Henry van Dyke (1852-1933)

NOT FOR ONE single day
    Can I discern my way,
      But this I surely know—
    Who gives the day
    Will show the way,
      So I securely go.

John Oxenham (1861-1941)

THERE IS A path in which every child of God is to walk, and in which alone God can accompany him.

Denham Smith

The Zigzag Path

We climbed the height by the zigzag path
And wondered why—until
We understood it was made zigzag
To break the force of the hill.

A road straight up would prove too steep
For the traveler's feet to tread;
The thought was kind in its wise design
Of a zigzag path instead.

It is often so in our daily life;
We fail to understand
That the twisting way our feet must tread
By love alone was planned.

Then murmur not at the winding way,
It is our Father's will
To lead us Home by the zigzag path,
To break the force of the hill.

Author Unknown

Two Ways

To every soul there openeth
   A high way and a low;
The high soul climbs the high way,
The low soul gropes the low,
And in between, on the misty flats,
The rest drift to and fro.

To every soul there openeth
A high way and a low;
And every man decideth
Which way his soul shall go.

John Oxenham (1861-1941)

Vestigia

I took a day to search for God
And found him not. But as I trod
   By rocky ledge, through woods untamed,
   Just where one scarlet lily flamed,
I saw his footprint in the sod.

Then suddenly, all unaware,
Far off in the deep shadows, where
   A solitary hermit thrush
   Sang through the holy twilight hush—
I heard his voice upon the air.

And even as I marveled how
God gives us heaven here and now,
   In a stir of wind that hardly shook
   The poplar leaves beside the brook—
His hand was light upon my brow.

At last with evening I turned
Homeward, and thought what I had learned
   And all that there was still to probe—
   I caught the glory of his robe
Where the last fires of sunset burned.

Back to the world with quickening start
I looked and longed for any part
   In making saving beauty be—
   And from that kindling ecstasy
I knew God dwelt within my heart.

Bliss Carman (1861-1929)

The Arrow And the Song

I shot an arrow into the air,
It fell to earth, I knew not where;
For, so swiftly it flew, the sight
Could not follow it in its flight.

I breathed a song into the air,
It fell to earth, I knew not where;
For who has sight so keen and strong,

That it can follow the flight of song?

Long, long afterward, in an oak
I found the arrow, still unbroke;
And the song, from beginning to end,
I found again in the heart of a friend.

Henry Wadsworth Longfellow (1807-1882)

Friends Old And New

Make new friends, but keep the old;
Those are silver, these are gold;
New-made friendships, like new wine,
Age will mellow and refine.
Friendships that have stood the test—
Time and change—are surely best;
Brow may wrinkle, hair grow gray,
Friendship never knows decay.

For 'mid old friends, tried and true,
Once more we our youth renew.
But old friends, alas! may die,
New friends must their place supply.
Cherish friendship in your breast;
New is good, but old is best;
Make new friends, but keep the old;
Those are silver, these are gold.

Author Unknown

God Bless Our Friendship

It is in loving, not in being loved
The heart finds its quest;
It is in giving, not in getting
Our lives are blest.

Author Unknown

A friend is a present you give yourself.
Robert Louis Stevenson (1850-1894)

FRIENDSHIP IS THE golden thread that ties the hearts of all the world.

John Evelyn (1620-1706)

A TRUE FRIEND is forever a friend.
George Macdonald (1824-1905)

A FRIEND LOVETH at all times, and a brother is born for adversity.

Proverbs 17:17

A MAN *THAT HATH FRIENDS* must shew himself friendly: and there is a friend *that* sticketh closer than a brother.

Proverbs 18:24

Thy Neighbor

Who is thy neighbor? He whom thou
Hast power to aid or bless;
Whose aching heart or burning brow
Thy soothing hand may press.
Thy neighbor? 'Tis the fainting poor
Whose eye with want is dim;
Oh, enter thou his humble door
With aid and peace for him.
Thy neighbor? He who drinks the cup
When sorrow drowns the brim;
With words of high sustaining hope
Go thou and comfort him.
Thy neighbor? 'Tis the weary slave,
Fettered in mind and limb;
He hath no hope this side the grave;
Go thou and ransom him.
Thy neighbor? Pass no mourner by;
Perhaps thou canst redeem
A breaking heart from misery;
Go share thy lot with him.

Author Unknown

The Search

No one could tell me where my soul might be;
I searched for God, and He eluded me;
I sought my brother out, and found all three.

Ernest Crosby (1856-1907)

The measure of a man's life is the well spending of it,
and not the length.

Plutarch (50-120 A.D.)

NO ONE IS useless in this world who lightens the burden of it to anyone else.

Charles Dickens (1812-1870)

OUR THOUGHT IS the key which unlocks the doors
of the world. There is something in us which corresponds
to that which is around us, beneath us, and above us.

Samuel McChord Crothers (1857-1927)

I Said A Prayer For You Today

I said a prayer for you today
And know God must have heard;
I felt the answer in my heart
Although He spoke not a word.
I didn't ask for wealth or fame
(I knew you wouldn't mind);
I asked for priceless treasures rare
Of a more lasting kind.
I prayed that He'd be near to you
At the start of each new day,
To grant you health and blessings fair,
And friends to share your way.
I asked for happiness for you
In all things great and small,
But that you'd know His loving care
I prayed the most of all.

Author Unknown

The Secret

I met God in the morning
When my day was at its best,
And His presence came like sunrise,
Like a glory in my breast.
All day long the Presence lingered,
All day long He stayed with me,
And we sailed in perfect calmness

O'er a very troubled sea.
Other ships were blown and battered,
Other ships were sore distressed,
But the winds that seemed to drive them
Brought to us a peace and rest.
Then I thought of other mornings,
With a keen remorse of mind,
When I too had loosed the moorings,
With the Presence left behind.
So I think I know the secret,
Learned from many a troubled way:
You must seek Him in the morning
If you want Him through the day!

Ralph Spaulding Cushman

The Master's Loom

M an's life is laid in the loom of time
To a pattern he does not see,
While the weavers work and the shuttles fly
Till the dawn of eternity.

Some shuttles are filled with silver threads
And some with threads of gold,
While often but the darker hues
Are all that they may hold.

But the weaver watches with skillful eye
Each shuttle fly to and fro,

And sees the pattern so deftly wrought
As the loom moves sure and slow.

God surely planned the pattern:
Each thread, the dark and fair,
Is chosen by His master skill
And placed in the web with care.

He only knows its beauty,
And guides the shuttles which hold
The threads so unattractive,
As well as the threads of gold.

Not till each loom is silent,
And the shuttles cease to fly,
Shall God reveal the pattern
And explain the reason why.

The dark threads were as needful
In the weaver's skillful hand
As the threads of gold and silver
For the pattern which He planned.

Author Unknown

The Weaver

I sat at my loom in silence,
Facing the western sun;
The warp was rough and tangled

And the threads unevenly run.
Impatiently I pulled at the fibers—
They snapped and flew from my hand;
Weary and faint and sore hearted
I gathered the broken strands.

I had beautiful colors to work with,
White, blue like heaven above,
And tangled in all the meshes
Were the golden threads of love;
But the colors were dulled by my handling,
The pattern was faded and gray,
That once to my eager seeming
Shone fairer than flowers of May.

But alas, not the half of my pattern
Was finished at set of sun;
What should I say to the Master
When I heard him call, "Is it done?"
I threw down my shuttle in sorrow
(I had worked through the livelong day)
And I lay down to slumber in darkness,
Too weary even to pray.

In my dreams a vision of splendor,
An angel, smiling faced,
With gentle and tender finger
The work of the weavers traced.
He stooped with a benediction

O'er the loom of my neighbor near,
For the threads were smooth and even
And the pattern perfect and clear.

Then I waited in fear and trembling,
As he stood by my tangled
   skein,
For the look of reproach—and pity—
That I knew would add to my pain.
Instead, with a thoughtful aspect,
He turned his gaze upon me,
And I knew that he saw the fair picture
Of my work as I hoped it would be.

And with touch divine of his finger
He traced my faint copy anew,
Transforming the clouded colors,
And letting the pattern shine true,
And I knew in that moment of waiting,
While his look pierced my very soul through,
I was judged not so much by my doing
As by what I had striven to do.

Author Unknown

Tapestry

My life is but a weaving, between my God and me,
I do not choose the colors, He worketh steadily,
Oft times He weaveth sorrow, and I in foolish pride,
Forget He sees the upper, and I the underside.

Not 'til the loom is silent, and shuttles cease to fly,
Will God unroll the canvas and explain the reason why.
The dark threads are as needful in the skillful Weaver's
    Hand,
As the threads of gold and silver in the pattern He has
    planned.

Author Unknown

My Old Bible

Though the cover is worn,
    And the pages are torn,
    And though places bear traces of tears,
Yet more precious than gold
Is this Book worn and old,
    That can shatter and scatter my fears.

This old Book is my guide,
'Tis a friend by my side,
    It will lighten and brighten my way;
And each promise I find
Soothes and gladdens the mind,
    As I read it and heed it each day.

To this Book I will cling,
Of its worth I will sing,
  Though great losses and crosses be mine;
For I cannot despair,
Though surrounded by care,
While possessing this blessing Divine.

Author Unknown

The Book Our Mothers Read

We search the world for truth; we cull
  The good, the pure, the beautiful,
From graven stone and written scroll,
From all old flower-fields of the soul;
And, weary seekers of the best,
We come back laden from the quest,
To find that all the sages said
Is in the Book our mothers read.

John Greenleaf Whittier (1807-1892)

The Bible

Within this ample volume lies
　　The mystery of mysteries.
Happiest they of human race
To whom their God has given grace
To read, to fear, to hope, to pray,
To lift the latch, to force the way;
But better had they ne'er been born
That read to doubt or read to scorn.

Sir Walter Scott (1771-1832)

What God Hath Promised!

God hath not promised
Skies always blue,
Flower-strewn pathways
All our lives through;
God hath not promised
Sun without rain,
Joy without sorrow,
Peace without pain.

But God hath promised
Strength for the day,
Rest for the labor,
Light for the way,
Grace for the trials,
Help from above,

Unfailing sympathy,
Undying Love.
Annie Johnson Flint

Overheard In an Orchard

Said the Robin to the Sparrow:
"I should really like to know
Why these anxious human beings
Rush about and worry so?"

Said the Sparrow to the Robin:
"Friend, I think that it must be
That they have no heavenly Father
Such as cares for you and me."
Elizabeth Cheney

Behold the fowls of the air: for they sow not, neither
do they reap, nor gather into barns; yet your heavenly Father feedeth them. Are ye not much better than
they?

Which of you by taking thought can add one cubit
unto his stature?

And why take ye thought for raiment? Consider the lilies of the field, how they grow; they toil not, neither do
they spin:

And yet I say unto you, That even Solomon in all his glory was not arrayed like one of these.

Wherefore, if God so clothe the grass of the field, which today is, and tomorrow is cast into the oven, shall he not much more clothe you, O ye of little faith?

Therefore take no thought, saying, What shall we eat? or, What shall we drink? or, Wherewithal shall we be clothed?...

But seek ye first the kingdom of God, and his righteousness; and all these things shall be added unto you.

Take therefore no thought for the morrow: for the morrow shall take thought for the things of itself.

Matthew 6:26-34

Out In the Fields With God

The little cares that fretted me
I lost them yesterday,
Among the fields above the sea,
Among the winds at play;
Among the lowing of the herds,
The rustling of the trees;
Among the singing of the birds,
The humming of the bees.

The foolish fears of what might happen,

I cast them all away
Among the clover-scented grass,
Among the new-mown hay;
Among the husking of the corn,
Where drowsy poppies nod,
Where ill thoughts die and good are born--
Out in the fields with God!

Elizabeth Barrett Browning (1806-1861)

I Shall Not Pass Again
This Way

The bread that giveth strength I want to give;
  The water pure that bids the thirsty live;
I want to help the fainting day by day,
Because I shall not pass again this way.

I want to give the oil of joy for tears;
The faith to conquer cruel doubts and fears;
Beauty for ashes may I give alway,
Because I shall not pass again this way.

I want to give good measure running o'er,
And into angry hearts I want to pour
The answer soft that turneth wrath away,
Because I shall not pass again this way.

I want to give to others hope and faith;

I want to do all that the Master saith;
I want to live aright from day to day,
Because I shall not pass again this way.

Author Unknown

Old Irish Verse

May the road rise up to meet you,
May the wind be always at your back,
May the sun shine warm upon your face,
And the rains fall soft upon your fields,
And until we meet again,
May God hold you in the palm of His hand.

Author Unknown

Do not look forward to the changes and chances of
this life in fear; rather look to them with full hope
that, as they arise, God, whose you are, will deliver you
out of them.

He is your Keeper. He has kept you hitherto. Do you
but hold fast to His dear hand, and He will lead you
safely through all things; and, when you cannot stand,
He will bear you in His arms.

Do not look forward to what may happen tomorrow.
Our Father will either shield you from suffering, or He
will give you strength to bear it.

Saint Francis of Sales (1567-1622)

More Favorites

More Favorites

More Favorites

More Favorites

Part Three

Treasured Hymns

A Mighty Fortress Is Our God

A mighty fortress is our God,
A bulwark never failing;
Our helper he amid the flood
Of mortal ills prevailing:
For still our ancient foe
Doth seek to work us woe;
His craft and pow'r are great,
And, armed with cruel hate,
On earth is not his equal.

Did we in our own strength confide,
Our striving would be losing;
Were not the right man on our side,
The man of God's own choosing:
Dost ask who that may be?
Christ Jesus, it is he;
Lord Sabaoth his Name,
From age to age the same,
And he must win the battle.

And tho' this world, with devils filled,
Should threaten to undo us;
We will not fear, for God hath willed
His truth to triumph through us:
The prince of darkness grim,
We tremble not for him;
His rage we can endure,

For lo! his doom is sure,
One little word shall fell him.

That word above all earthly pow'rs,
No thanks to them, abideth;
The Spirit and the gifts are ours
Through him who with us sideth:
Let goods and kindred go,
This mortal life also;
The body they may kill:
God's truth abideth still,
His kingdom is forever.

Martin Luther (1483-1546)

A Wonderful Saviour Is Jesus My Lord

A wonderful Saviour is Jesus my Lord,
A wonderful Saviour to me;
He hideth my soul in the cleft of the rock,
Where rivers of pleasure I see.

Refrain:
   He hideth my soul in the cleft of the rock,
   That shadows a dry, thirsty land;
   He hideth my life in the depths of his love,
   And covers me there with his hand,
   And covers me there with his hand.

A wonderful Saviour is Jesus my Lord,
He taketh my burden away;
He holdeth me up, and I shall not be moved;
He giveth me strength as my day.

With numberless blessings each moment he crowns,
And filled with his fullness divine,
I sing in my rapture, "Oh, glory to God
For such a Redeemer as mine!"

When clothed in his brightness transported I rise
To meet him in clouds of the sky,
His perfect salvation, his wonderful love,
I'll shout with the millions on high.

Fanny J. Crosby (1820-1915)

Abide With Me

A bide with me: fast falls the eventide,
The darkness deepens—Lord, with me abide!
When other helpers fail, and comforts flee,
Help of the helpless, O abide with me!

Swift to its close ebbs out life's little day;
Earth's joys grow dim, its glories pass away;
Change and decay in all around I see;
O thou, who changest not abide with me!

I need thy presence ev'ry passing hour;
What but thy grace can foil the tempter's pow'r?
Who, like thyself, my guide and stay can be?
Thro' cloud and sunshine, Lord, abide with me.

I fear no foe, with thee at hand to bless;
Ills have no weight, and tears no bitterness;
Where is death's sting? where, grave, thy victory?
I triumph still, if thou abide with me.

Hold thou thy cross before my closing eyes;
Shine thro' the gloom and point me to the skies;
Heav'n's morning breaks, and earth's vain shadows flee;
In life, in death, O Lord, abide with me!

Henry Francis Lyte (1793-1847)

All the Way My Saviour Leads Me

All the way my Saviour leads me;
   What have I to ask beside?
Can I doubt his tender mercy
   Who thro' life has been my guide?
Heav'nly peace, divinest comfort,
   Here by faith in him to dwell!

For I know, whate'er befall me, Jesus doeth all things
   well;
For I know, whate'er befall me, Jesus doeth all things
   well.

All the way my Saviour leads me;
   Cheers each winding path I tread;
Gives me grace for ev'ry trial,
   Feeds me with the living bread;
Tho' my weary steps may falter,
   And my soul athirst may be,
Gushing from the Rock before me, Lo! a spring of joy I
   see;
Gushing from the Rock before me, Lo! a spring of joy I
   see.

All the way my Saviour leads me;
   O the fullness of his love!
Perfect rest to me is promised
   In my Father's house above;
When my spirit, clothed immortal,
   Wings its flight to realms of day,
This my song thro' endless ages, Jesus led me all the way;
This my song thro' endless ages, Jesus led me all the way.

Fanny J. Crosby (1820-1915)

Amazing Grace

Amazing grace! how sweet the sound,
That saved a wretch like me!
I once was lost, but now am found,
Was blind, but now I see.

'Twas grace that taught my heart to fear,
And grace my fears relieved;
How precious did that grace appear
The hour I first believed!

Thro' many dangers, toils and snares,
I have already come;
'Tis grace hath brought me safe thus far,
And grace will lead me home.

The Lord has promised good to me,
His Word my hope secures;
He will my shield and portion be
As long as life endures.

The earth shall soon dissolve like snow,
The sun forbear to shine;
But God, who called me here below,
Will be forever mine.

John Newton (1725-1807)

Be Still, My Soul

Be still, my soul: the Lord is on thy side;
Bear patiently the cross of grief or pain;
Leave to thy God to order and provide;
In ev'ry change he faithful will remain.
Be still, my soul: thy best, thy heav'nly Friend
Thro' thorny ways leads to a joyful end.

Be still, my soul: thy God doth undertake
To guide the future as he has the past,
Thy hope, thy confidence let nothing shake;
All now mysterious shall be bright at last.
Be still, my soul: the waves and winds still know
His voice who ruled them while he dwelt below.

Be still, my soul: the hour is hast'ning on
When we shall be forever with the Lord,
When disappointment, grief, and fear are gone,
Sorrow forgot, love's purest joys restored.
Be still, my soul: when change and tears are past,
All safe and blessed we shall meet at last.

Katharina von Schlegel (1697-?)

Beneath the Cross Of Jesus

Beneath the cross of Jesus I fain would take my stand,
The shadow of a mighty rock within a weary land;
A home within the wilderness, a rest upon the way,
From the burning of the noontide heat, and the burden of
the day.

Upon that cross of Jesus mine eye at times can see
The very dying form of One Who suffered there for me;
And from my stricken heart with tears two wonders I
confess:
The wonders of his glorious love and my unworthiness.

I take, O cross, thy shadow for my abiding place;
I ask no other sunshine than the sunshine of his face;
Content to let the world go by, to know no gain nor loss,
My sinful self my only shame, my glory all the cross.

Elizabeth C. Clephane (1830-1869)

Blessed Assurance

Blessed assurance, Jesus is mine!
Oh, what a foretaste of glory divine!
Heir of salvation, purchase of God,
Born of his Spirit, washed in his blood.

Refrain:
    This is my story, this is my song,
    Praising my Saviour all the day long;
    This is my story, this is my song,
    Praising my Saviour all the day long.

Perfect submission, perfect delight,
Visions of rapture now burst on my sight;
Angels, descending, bring from above,
Echoes of mercy, whispers of love.

Perfect submission, all is at rest,
I in my Saviour am happy and blest;
Watching and waiting, looking above,
Filled with his goodness, lost in his love.

Fanny J. Crosby (1820-1915)

Breathe On Me, Breath Of God

Breathe on me, breath of God,
    Fill me with life anew,
That I may love what thou dost love,
    And do what thou wouldst do.

Breathe on me, breath of God,
    Until my heart is pure,
Until with thee I will one will,

To do and to endure.

Breathe on me, breath of God,
Till I am wholly thine,
Until this earthly part of me
Glows with thy fire divine.

Breathe on me, Breath of God,
So shall I never die,
But live with thee the perfect life
Of thine eternity.

Edwin Hatch (1835-1889)

Come, Thou Almighty King

Come, thou almighty King,
Help us thy Name to sing,
Help us to praise! Father all glorious,
O'er all victorious,
Come, and reign over us,
Ancient of Days!

Come, thou Incarnate Word,
Gird on thy mighty sword,
Our pray'r attend; Come, and thy people bless,
And give thy word success;
Spirit of holiness,
On us descend!

Come, Holy Comforter,
Thy sacred witness bear,
In this glad hour: Thou who almighty art,
Now rule in every heart,
And ne'er from us depart,
Spirit of power!

To thee, great One in Three,
Eternal praises be
Hence, evermore: Thy sov'reign majesty
May we in glory see,
And to eternity
Love and adore!

Author Unknown

Fairest Lord Jesus

Fairest Lord Jesus, Ruler of all nature,
O thou of God and man the Son,
Thee will I cherish, Thee will I honor,
Thee, my soul's Glory, Joy, and Crown.

Fair are the meadows, Fairer still the woodlands,
Robed in the blooming garb of spring:
Jesus is fairer, Jesus is purer,
Who makes the woeful heart to sing.

Fair is the sunshine, Fairer still the moonlight,

And all the twinkling starry host:
Jesus shines brighter, Jesus shines purer
Than all the angels heaven can boast.

German, 17th Century

Father, Lead Me Day By Day

Father, lead me day by day,
Ever in thine own good way;
Teach me to be pure and true,
Show me what I ought to do.

When in danger, make me brave,
Make me know that thou canst save;
Keep me safely by thy side;
Let me in thy love abide.

When I'm tempted to do wrong,
Make me steadfast, wise, and strong;
And when all alone I stand,
Shield me with thy mighty hand.

May I do the good I know,
Serving gladly here below;
Then at last go home to thee,
Evermore thine own to be.

John P. Hopps (1834-1911)

For the Beauty Of the Earth

For the beauty of the earth;
For the glory of the skies;
For the love which from our birth
Over and around us lies:
Lord of all, to thee we raise
This our hymn of grateful praise.

For the wonder of each hour
Of the day and of the night,
Hill and vale, and tree and flower,
Sun and moon, and stars of light:
Lord of all, to thee we raise
This our hymn of grateful praise.

For the joy of ear and eye;
For the heart and mind's delight;
For the mystic harmony
Linking sense to sound and sight:
Lord of all, to thee we raise
This our hymn of grateful praise.

For the joy of human love,
Brother, sister, parent, child,
Friends on earth, and friends above;
For all gentle thoughts and mild:
Lord of all, to thee we raise
This our hymn of grateful praise.

For thy Church that evermore
Lifteth holy hands above,
Offering up on every shore
Her pure sacrifice of love:
Lord of all, to thee we raise
This our hymn of grateful praise.

Folliott S. Pierpoint (1835-1917)

Give Of Your Best To the Master

Give of your best to the Master:
Give of the strength of your youth;
Throw your soul's fresh, glowing ardor
Into the battle for truth.
Jesus has set the example;
Dauntless was he, young and brave;
Give him your loyal devotion,
Give him the best that you have.

Refrain:
    Give of your best to the Master;
    Give of the strength of your youth;
    Clad in salvation's full armor,
    Join in the battle for truth.

Give of your best to the Master;
Give him first place in your heart;

Give him first place in your service,
Consecrate ev'ry part.
Give, and to you shall be given;
God his beloved Son gave;
Gratefully seeking to serve him,
Give him the best that you have.

Give of your best to the Master;
Naught else is worthy his love;
He gave himself for your ransom,
Gave up his glory above:
Laid down his life without murmur,
You from sin's ruin to save;
Give him your heart's adoration,
Give him the best that you have.

Howard B. Grose

Glorious Things Of Thee Are Spoken

G lorious things of thee are spoken,
Zion, city of our God;
He whose word cannot be broken
Formed thee for his own abode:
On the Rock of Ages founded,
What can shake thy sure repose?
With salvation's walls surrounded,
Thou mayst smile at all thy foes.

See, the streams of living waters,
Springing from eternal love,
Still supply thy sons and daughters,
And all fear of want remove:
Who can faint while such a river
Ever flows our thirst to assuage?
Grace, which, like the Lord the Giver,
Never fails from age to age.
Round each habitation hov'ring,
See the cloud and fire appear
For a glory and a cov'ring,
Showing that the Lord is near:

He who gives us daily manna,
He who listens when we cry,
Let him hear the loud Hosanna
Rising to his throne on high.

John Newton (1725-1807)

He Leadeth Me:
O Blessed Thought

He leadeth me: O blessed thought!
O words with heav'nly comfort fraught!
Whate'er I do, where'er I be,
Still 'tis God's hand that leadeth me.

Refrain:
  He leadeth me! He leadeth me!
  By his own hand he leadeth me:
  His faithful follow'r I would be,
  For by his hand he leadeth me.

Sometimes 'mid scenes of deepest gloom,
Sometimes where Eden's bowers bloom,
By waters still, o'er troubled sea—
Still 'tis his hand that leadeth me.

Lord! I would clasp thy hand in mine,
Nor ever murmur nor repine;
Content, whatever lot I see,

Since 'tis my God that leadeth me.

And when my task on earth is done,
When, by thy grace the vict'ry's won,
E'en death's cold wave I will not flee,
Since God thro' Jordan leadeth me.

Joseph H. Gilmore (1834-1918)

Holy, Holy, Holy! Lord God Almighty

Holy, holy, holy! Lord God Almighty!
Early in the morning
  our song shall rise to thee;
Holy, holy, holy, merciful and mighty,
God in Three Persons, blessed Trinity!

Holy, holy, holy! all the saints adore thee,
Casting down their golden crowns
  around the glassy sea;
Cherubim and seraphim falling down before thee,
Which wert, and art, and evermore shalt be.

Holy, holy, holy! tho' the darkness hide thee,
Tho' the eye of sinful man
  thy glory may not see;
Only thou art holy! there is none beside thee,
Perfect in pow'r, in love and purity!

Holy, holy, holy! Lord God Almighty!
All thy works shall praise thy name,
   in earth and sky and sea;
Holy, holy, holy, merciful and mighty,
God in Three Persons, blessed Trinity!

Reginald Heber (1783-1826)

How Firm a Foundation,
Ye Saints Of the Lord

How firm a foundation, ye saints of the Lord,
Is laid for your faith in his excellent Word!
What more can he say than to you he hath said,
To you who for refuge to Jesus have fled?
To you who for refuge to Jesus have fled?

"Fear not, I am with thee, O be not dismayed;
For I am thy God, and will still give thee aid;
I'll strengthen thee, help thee and cause thee to stand,
Upheld by my gracious omnipotent hand,
Upheld by my gracious omnipotent hand.

"When thro' the deep waters I call thee to go,
The rivers of sorrow shall not overflow;
For I will be with thee thy trials to bless,
And sanctify to thee thy deepest distress,
And sanctify to thee thy deepest distress.

"E'en down to old age all my people shall prove
My sov'reign, eternal, unchangeable love;
And when hoary hairs shall their temples adorn,
Like lambs they shall still in my bosom be borne,
Like lambs they shall still in my bosom be borne.

"The soul that on Jesus hath leaned for repose,
I will not, I will not desert to his foes;
That soul, though all hell should endeavor to shake,
I'll never, no, never, no, never forsake,
I'll never, no, never, no, never forsake."

"K" in Rippon's Selection, 1787

I Know That My Redeemer Lives

I know that my Redeemer lives;
He lives, who once was dead;
To me in grief he comfort gives;
With peace he crowns my head.

He lives triumphant o'er the grave,
At God's right hand on high,
My ransomed soul to keep and save,
To bless and glorify.

He lives, that I may also live,
And now his grace proclaim;
He lives, that I may honor give
To his most holy Name.

Let strains of heav'nly music rise,
While all their anthem sing
To Christ, my precious sacrifice,
And everliving King.

Charles Wesley (1707-1788)

I Sing the Mighty Power Of God

I sing the mighty power of God,
That made the mountains rise;
That spread the flowing seas abroad,
And built the lofty skies.
I sing the Wisdom that ordained
The sun to rule the day;
The moon shines full at his command,
And all the stars obey.

I sing the goodness of the Lord,
That filled the earth with food;
He formed the creatures with his word,

And then pronounced them good.
Lord, how thy wonders are displayed,
Where'er I turn my eye:
If I survey the ground I tread,
Or gaze upon the sky!

There's not a plant or flower below,
But makes thy glories known;
And clouds arise, and tempests blow,
By order from thy throne;
While all that borrows life from thee
Is ever in thy care,
And everywhere that man can be,
Thou, God, art present there.

Sir Isaac Watts (1674-1748)

In Heavenly Love Abiding

In heav'nly love abiding,
No change my heart shall fear;
And safe is such confiding,
For nothing changes here.
The storm may roar without me,
My heart may low be laid,
But God is round about me,
And can I be dismayed?

Wherever he may guide me,
No want shall turn me back;
My Shepherd is beside me,
And nothing can I lack.
His wisdom ever waketh,
His sight is never dim;
He knows the way he taketh,
And I will walk with him.

Green pastures are before me,
Which yet I have not seen;
Bright skies will soon be o'er me,
Where the dark clouds have been.
My hope I cannot measure,
My path to life is free;
My Saviour has my treasure,
And he will walk with me.

Anna L. Waring (1820-1910)

In the Cross Of Christ I Glory

In the cross of Christ I glory,
Tow'ring o'er the wrecks of time;
All the light of sacred story
Gathers round its head sublime.

When the woes of life o'ertake me
Hopes deceive, and fears annoy,
Never shall the cross forsake me;
Lo! it glows with peace and joy.

When the sun of bliss is beaming
Light and love upon my way,
From the cross the radiance streaming
Adds more luster to the day.

Bane and blessing, pain and pleasure,
By the cross are sanctified;
Peace is there that knows no measure,
Joys that through all time abide.

John Bowring (1792-1872)

In the Garden

I come to the garden alone,
While the dew is still on the roses;
And the voice I hear, falling on my ear,
The Son of God discloses.

Refrain
    And He walks with me, and He talks with me,
    And He tells I am His own;
    And the joy we share as we tarry there,
    None other has ever known.

He speaks, and the sound of His voice
Is so sweet the birds hush their singing,
And the melody that He gave to me
Within my heart is ringing.

I'd stay in the garden with Him
Though the night around me be falling,
But He bids me go; through the voice of woe,
His voice to me is calling.

C. Austin Miles (1868-1946)

It Is Well With My Soul

When peace like a river attendeth my way,
When sorrows like sea billows roll;
Whatever my lot, thou hast taught me to say,
"It is well, it is well with my soul."

Refrain:
  It is well with my soul;
  It is well, it is well with my soul.

Tho' Satan should buffet, tho' trials should come,
Let this blest assurance control,
That Christ hath regarded my helpless estate,
And hath shed his own blood for my soul.

My sin—O the bliss of the glorious tho't!
My sin—not in part, but the whole,
Is nailed to his cross and I bear it no more;
Praise the Lord, praise the Lord, O my soul!

And, Lord, haste the day when the faith shall be
    sight,
The clouds be rolled back as a scroll,
The trump shall resound, and the Lord shall
    descend;
"Even so"—it is well with my soul.

Henry G. Spafford

Jesus, Keep Me Near the Cross

Jesus, keep me near the cross;
  There a precious fountain,
Free to all—a healing stream—
Flows from Calv'ry's mountain.

Refrain:
    In the cross, in the cross,
    Be my glory ever,
    Till my raptured soul shall find
    Rest beyond the river.

Near the cross, a trembling soul,
Love and mercy found me;
There the bright and morning Star
Shed its beams around me.

Near the cross! O Lamb of God,
Bring its scenes before me;
Help me walk from day to day
With its shadow o'er me.

Near the cross I'll watch and wait,
Hoping, trusting ever,
Till I reach the golden strand
Just beyond the river.

Fanny J. Crosby (1820-1915)

Jesus, Lover Of My Soul

Jesus, Lover of my soul,
  Let me to thy bosom fly,
While the nearer waters roll,
While the tempest still is high.
Hide me, O my Saviour, hide,
Till the storm of life is past;
Safe into the haven guide;
O receive my soul at last!

Other refuge have I none;
Hangs my helpless soul on thee;
Leave, O leave me not alone,
Still support and comfort me.
All my trust on thee is stayed,
All my help from thee I bring;
Cover my defenseless head
With the shadow of thy wing.

Thou, O Christ, art all I want;
More than all in thee I find;
Raise the fallen, cheer the faint,
Heal the sick, and lead the blind.
Just and holy is thy name;
I am all unrighteousness;
False and full of sin I am,
Thou art full of truth and grace.

Plenteous grace with thee is found,
Grace to cover all my sin;
Let the healing streams abound;
Make and keep me pure within.
Thou of life the Fountain art,
Freely let me take of thee;
Spring thou up within my heart,
Rise to all eternity.

Charles Wesley (1707-1788)

Jesus, Saviour, Pilot Me

Jesus, Saviour, pilot me
  Over life's tempestuous sea;
Unknown waves before me roll,
Hiding rock and treach'rous shoal,
Chart and compass came from thee:
Jesus, Saviour, pilot me.

As a mother stills her child,
Thou canst hush the ocean wild;
Boist'rous waves obey thy will
When thou sayest to them "Be still."
Wondrous Sov'reign of the sea,
Jesus, Saviour, pilot me.

When at last I near the shore,
And the fearful breakers roar
'Twist me and the peaceful rest,
Then, while leaning on thy breast,
May I hear thee say to me,
"Fear not, I will pilot thee."

Edward Hopper (1818-1888)

Jesus, the Very Thought
Of Thee

Jesus, the very tho't of thee
   With sweetness fills my breast;
But sweeter far thy face to see,
And in thy presence rest.

No voice can sing, no heart can frame,
Nor can the mem'ry find
A sweeter sound than thy blest name,
O Saviour of mankind!

O Hope of ev'ry contrite heart,
O Joy of all the meek,
To those who fall, how kind thou art!
How good to those who seek!

Jesus, our only Joy be thou,
As thou our Prize wilt be;
Jesus, be thou our Glory now,
And thro' eternity.

Ascribed to Bernard of Clairvaux (1091-1153)

Joyful, Joyful, We Adore Thee

Joyful, joyful, we adore thee,
  God of glory, Lord of love;
Hearts unfold like flowers before thee,
Opening to the sun above.
Melt the clouds of sin and sadness,
Drive the dark of doubt away;
Giver of immortal gladness,
Fill us with the light of day.

All thy works with joy surround thee,
Earth and heaven reflect thy rays,
Stars and angels sing around thee,
Center of unbroken praise.
Field and forest, vale and mountain,
Flowery meadow, flashing sea,
Chanting bird and flowing fountain,
Call us to rejoice in thee.

Thou art giving and forgiving,
Ever blessing, ever blest,
Wellspring of the joy of living,

Ocean depth of happy rest!
Thou our Father, Christ our Brother,
All who live in love are thine;
Teach us how to love each other,
Lift us to the Joy divine.

Henry van Dyke (1852-1933)

Love Divine, All Love's Excelling

L ove divine, all loves excelling,
Joy of heav'n to earth come down,
Fix in us thy humble dwelling;
All thy faithful mercies crown.
Jesus, thou art all compassion,
Pure, unbounded love thou art;
Visit us with thy salvation;
Enter ev'ry trembling heart.

Breathe, O breathe thy loving Spirit
Into ev'ry troubled breast:
Let us all in thee inherit;
Let us find that second rest.
Take away our bent to sinning;
Alpha and Omega be;
End of faith as its beginning,
Set our hearts at liberty.

Come, almighty to deliver,
Let us all thy life receive;
Suddenly return, and never,
Nevermore thy temples leave:
Thee we would be always blessing,
Serve thee as thy hosts above,
Pray, and praise thee without ceasing,
Glory in thy perfect love.

Finish then thy new creation;
Pure and spotless let us be;
Let us see thy great salvation,
Perfectly restored in thee:
Changed from glory into glory,
Till in heav'n we take our place,
Till we cast our crowns before thee,
Lost in wonder, love and praise.

Charles Wesley (1707-1788)

Must Jesus Bear the Cross Alone

Must Jesus bear the cross alone
And all the world go free?
No; there's a cross for ev'ryone,
And there's a cross for me.

The consecrated cross I'll bear
Till death shall set me free,
And then go home my crown to wear,
For there's a crown for me.

Upon the crystal pavement, down
At Jesus' pierced feet,
Joyful, I'll cast my golden crown,
And his dear name repeat.

O precious cross! O glorious crown!
O resurrection day!
Ye angels, from the stars come down,
And bear my soul away.

Thomas Shepherd (1665-1739)

My Faith Looks Up To Thee

M y faith looks up to thee,
Thou Lamb of Calvary, Saviour divine!
Now hear me while I pray;
Take all my guilt away;
O let me from this day be wholly thine!

May thy rich grace impart
Strength to my fainting heart, my zeal inspire;
As thou hast died for me,
O may my love to thee

Pure, warm and changeless be, a living fire!

While life's dark maze I tread
And griefs around me spread, be thou my Guide;
Bid darkness turn to day;
Wipe sorrow's tears away,
Nor let me ever stray from thee aside.

When ends life's transient dream;
When death's cold, sullen stream shall o'er me roll;
Blest Saviour, then in love,
Fear and distrust remove;
O bear me safe above, a ransomed soul!

Ray Palmer (1808-1887)

Nearer, My God, To Thee

Nearer, my God, to thee,
Nearer to thee!
E'en though it be a cross
That raiseth me;
Still all my song shall be,
Nearer, my God, to thee,
Nearer, my God, to thee,
Nearer to thee!

Though like the wanderer,
The sun gone down,

Darkness be over me,
My rest a stone;
Yet in my dreams I'd be
Nearer, my God, to thee,
Nearer, my God, to thee,
Nearer to thee!

There let the way appear
Steps unto heaven:
All that thou sendest me
In mercy giv'n:
Angels to beckon me
Nearer, my God, to thee,
Nearer, my God, to thee,
Nearer to thee!

Then, with my waking thoughts
Bright with thy praise,
Out of my stony griefs
Bethel I'll raise;
So by my woes to be
Nearer, my God, to thee,
Nearer, my God, to thee,
Nearer to thee!

Or if on joyful wing
Cleaving the sky,
Sun, moon, and stars forgot,
Upward I fly,

Still all my song shall be,
Nearer, my God, to thee,
Nearer, my God, to thee,
Nearer to thee!

Sarah F. Adams (1805-1848)

O Could I Speak the Matchless Worth

O could I speak the matchless worth,
O could I sound the glories forth
Which in my Saviour shine,
I'd soar and touch the heav'nly strings,
And vie with Gabriel while he sings
In notes almost divine,
In notes almost divine.

I'd sing the precious blood he spilt,
My ransom from the dreadful guilt
Of sin and wrath divine;
I'd sing his glorious righteousness,
In which all perfect, heav'nly dress
My soul shall ever shine,
My soul shall ever shine.

I'd sing the characters he bears,
And all the forms of love he wears,

Exalted on this throne;
In loftiest songs of sweetest praise,
I would to everlasting days
Make all his glories known,
Make all his glories known.

Well, the delightful day will come
When my dear Lord will bring me home,
And I shall see his face;
Then with my Saviour, Brother, Friend,
A blest eternity I'll spend,
Triumphant in his grace,
Triumphant in his grace.

Samuel Medley (1738-1799)

O For A Faith That Will Not Shrink

O for a faith that will not shrink,
Tho' pressed by ev'ry foe,
That will not tremble on the brink
Of any earthly woe!

That will not murmur or complain
Beneath the chast'ning rod,
But, in the hour of grief or pain,
Will lean upon its God.

A faith that shines more bright and clear
When tempests rage without;
That when in danger knows no fear,
In darkness feels no doubt.

That bears, unmoved, the world's dread frown,
Nor heeds its scornful smile;
That seas of trouble cannot drown,
Nor Satan's arts beguile.

Lord, give us such a faith as this,
And then, whate'er may come,
We'll taste, e'en here, the hallowed bliss
Of an eternal home.

William H. Bathurst (1796-1877)

O For A Thousand
Tongues To Sing

O for a thousand tongues to sing
My great Redeemer's praise,
The glories of my God and King,
The triumphs of his grace!

My gracious Master and my God,
Assist me to proclaim,

To spread thro' all the earth abroad
The honors of thy name.

Jesus! the name that charms our fears,
That bids our sorrows cease,
'Tis music in the sinner's ears,
'Tis life, and health, and peace.

He breaks the power of canceled sin,
He sets the pris'ner free;
His blood can make the foulest clean;
His blood availed for me.

He speaks, and listening to his voice,
New life the dead receive;
The mournful, broken hearts rejoice;
The humble poor believe.

Hear him, ye deaf; his praise, ye dumb,
Your loosened tongues employ;
Ye blind, behold your Saviour come;
And leap, ye lame, for joy.

Charles Wesley (1707-1788)

O Love That Wilt Not Let Me Go

O Love that wilt not let me go,
I rest my weary soul in thee;
I give thee back the life I owe,
That in thine ocean depths its flow
May richer, fuller be.

O Light that follow'st all my way,
I yield my flick'ring torch to thee;
My heart restores its borrowed ray,
That in thy sunshine's blaze its day
May brighter, fairer be.

O Joy that seekest me through pain,
I cannot close my heart to thee;
I trace the rainbow thro' the rain,
And feel the promise is not vain
That morn shall tearless be.

O Cross that liftest up my head,
I dare not ask to fly from thee;
I lay in dust life's glory dead,
And from the ground there blossoms red
Life that shall endless be.

George Matheson (1842-1906)

O Master, Let Me Walk With Thee

O Master, let me walk with thee
In lowly paths of service free;
Tell me thy secret; help me bear
The strain of toil, the fret of care.

Help me the slow of heart to move
By some clear, winning word of love;
Teach me the wayward feet to stay,
And guide them in the homeward way.

Teach me thy patience; still with thee
In closer, dearer company,
In work that keeps faith sweet and strong,
In trust that triumphs over wrong.

In hope that sends a shining ray
Far down the future's broad'ning way;
In peace that only thou canst give,
With thee, O Master, let me live.

Washington Gladden (1836-1918)

O Worship the King

O worship the King all glorious above,
  And gratefully sing his wonderful love;
Our Shield and Defender, the Ancient of Days,
Pavilioned in splendor and girded with praise.

O tell of his might, and sing of his grace,
Whose robe is the light, whose canopy space;
His chariots of wrath the deep thunderclouds form,
And dark is his path on the wings of the storm.

Thy bountiful care what tongue can recite?
It breathes in the air, it shines in the light;
It streams from the hills, it descends to the plain,
And sweetly distils in the dew and the rain.

Frail children of dust, and feeble as frail,
In thee do we trust, nor find thee to fail;
Thy mercies how tender! how firm to the end!
Our Maker, Defender, Redeemer and Friend.

Robert Grant (1785-1838)

Praise To the Lord, the Almighty

Praise to the Lord, the Almighty, the King of creation!
O my soul, praise him, for he is thy health and
salvation!
All ye who hear,
Now to his temple draw near;
Join me in glad adoration!

Praise to the Lord, who o'er all things so wondrously
reigneth,
Shieldeth thee under his wings, yea, so gently sustaineth!
Hast thou not seen
How thy desires e'er have been
Granted in what he ordaineth?

Praise to the Lord, who doth prosper thy work and de-
fend thee;
Surely his goodness and mercy here daily attend thee.
Ponder anew
What the Almighty can do,
If with his love he befriend thee.

Joachim Neander (1650-1680)

Rock Of Ages, Cleft For Me

Rock of ages, cleft for me,
Let me hide myself in thee;
Let the water and the blood,
From thy wounded side which flowed,
Be of sin the double cure,
Save from wrath and make me pure.

Could my tears forever flow,
Could my zeal no languor know,
These for sin could not atone;
Thou must save and thou alone:
In my hand no price I bring;
Simply to the cross I cling.

While I draw this fleeting breath,
When my eyes shall close in death,
When I rise to worlds unknown,
And behold thee on thy throne,
Rock of ages, cleft for me,
Let me hide myself in thee.

Augustus Montague Toplady (1740-1778)

Saviour, Like a Shepherd Lead Us

Saviour, like a shepherd lead us,
Much we need thy tender care;
In thy pleasant pastures feed us,
For our use thy folds prepare:
Blessed Jesus, Blessed Jesus,
Thou hast bought us, thine we are;
Blessed Jesus, Blessed Jesus,
Thou hast bought us, thine we are.

We are thine; do thou befriend us,
Be the Guardian of our way;
Keep thy flock, from sin defend us,
Seek us when we go astray:
Blessed Jesus, Blessed Jesus,
Hear, O hear us when we pray;
Blessed Jesus, Blessed Jesus,
Hear, O hear us when we pray.

Thou hast promised to receive us,
Poor and sinful though we be;
Thou hast mercy to relieve us,
Grace to cleanse, and power to free:
Blessed Jesus, Blessed Jesus,
Early let us turn to thee;
Blessed Jesus, Blessed Jesus,
Early let us turn to thee.

Early let us seek thy favor;
Early let us do thy will;
Blessed Lord and only Saviour,
With thy love our bosoms fill:
Blessed Jesus, Blessed Jesus,
Thou hast loved us, love us still;
Blessed Jesus, Blessed Jesus,
Thou hast loved us, love us still.

Dorothy A. Thrupp (1779-1847)

Stand Up, Stand Up For Jesus

Stand up, stand up for Jesus!
Ye soldiers of the cross;
Lift high his royal banner,
It must not suffer loss;
From vict'ry unto vict'ry
His army shall he lead,
Till ev'ry foe is vanquished,
And Christ is Lord indeed.

Stand up, stand up for Jesus!
The trumpet call obey;
Forth to the mighty conflict
In this his glorious day.
Ye that are men now serve him
Against unnumbered foes;

Let courage rise with danger
And strength to strength oppose.

Stand up, stand up for Jesus!
Stand in his strength alone;
The arm of flesh will fail you;
Ye dare not trust your own;
Put on the gospel armor,
Each piece put on with prayer,
Where duty calls or danger
Be never wanting there.

Stand up, stand up for Jesus!
The strife will not be long;
This day the noise of battle,
The next the victor's song:
To him that overcometh,
A crown of life shall be;
He with the King of glory
Shall reign eternally.

George Duffield (1818-1888)

Still, Still With Thee

Still, still with thee, when purple morning breaketh,
When the bird waketh, and the shadows flee,
Fairer than morning, lovelier than daylight,
Dawns the sweet consciousness, I am with thee.

Alone with thee, amid the mystic shadows,
The solemn hush of nature newly born,
Alone with thee in breathless adoration,
In the calm dew and freshness of the morn.

Still, still with thee! As to each newborn morning
A fresh and solemn splendor still is given,
So does this blessed consciousness, awaking,
Breathe each day nearness unto thee and heaven.

So shall it be at last, in that bright morning,
When the soul waketh and life's shadows flee;
O in that hour, fairer than daylight dawning,
Shall rise the glorious thought, I am with thee.

Harriet Beecher Stowe (1812-1896)

Sweet Hour Of Prayer

Sweet hour of prayer! Sweet hour of prayer!
That calls me from a world of care,
And bids me at my Father's throne
Make all my wants and wishes known;
In seasons of distress and grief
My soul has often found relief,
And oft escaped the tempter's snare,
By thy return, sweet hour of prayer!

Sweet hour of prayer! Sweet hour of prayer!
The joys I feel, the bliss I share,
Of those whose anxious spirits burn
With strong desires for thy return!
With such I hasten to the place
Where God my Saviour shows his face,
And gladly take my station there,
And wait for thee, sweet hour of prayer!

Sweet hour of prayer! Sweet hour of prayer!
Thy wings shall my petition bear
To him whose truth and faithfulness
Engage the waiting soul to bless;
And since he bids me seek his face,
Believe his Word and trust his grace,
I'll cast on him my ev'ry care,
And wait for thee, sweet hour of prayer!

Sweet hour of prayer! Sweet hour of prayer!
May I thy consolation share,
Till, from Mount Pisgah's lofty height,
I view my home, and take my flight:
This robe of flesh I'll drop and rise
To seize the everlasting prize,
And shout, while passing through the air,
Farewell, farewell, sweet hour of prayer!

William Walford (1772-1850)

Take My Life And Let It Be

Take my life and let it be
Consecrated, Lord, to thee;
Take my moments and my days;
Let them flow in ceaseless praise,
Let them flow in ceaseless praise.

Take my hands and let them move
At the impulse of thy love;
Take my feet and let them be
Swift and beautiful for thee,
Swift and beautiful for thee.

Take my voice and let me sing,
Always, only, for my King.
Take my lips and let them be

Filled with messages from thee,
Filled with messages from thee.

Take my silver and my gold;
Not a mite would I withhold;
Take my intellect and use
Ev'ry power as thou shalt choose,
Ev'ry power as thou shalt choose.

Take my will and make it thine,
It shall be no longer mine;
Take my heart, it is thine own,
It shall be thy royal throne.
It shall be thy royal throne.

Take my love, my Lord, I pour
At thy feet its treasure store;
Take myself, and I will be
Ever, only, all for thee.
Ever, only, all for thee.

Frances Ridley Havergal (1836-1879)

Take Time To Be Holy

Take time to be holy,
Speak oft with thy Lord;
Abide in him always,
And feed on his Word;
Make friends of God's children,
Help those who are weak,
Forgetting in nothing
His blessing to seek.

Take time to be holy,
The world rushes on;
Spend much time in secret
With Jesus alone;
By looking to Jesus,
Like him thou shalt be;
Thy friends in thy conduct
His likeness shall see.

Take time to be holy,
Let him be thy guide,
And run not before him,
Whatever betide;
In joy or in sorrow,
Still follow thy Lord,
And, looking to Jesus,
Still trust in his word.

Take time to be holy, Be calm in thy soul;
Each tho't and each motive
Beneath his control;
Thus led by his Spirit
To fountains of love,
Thou soon shalt be fitted
For service above.

William Longstaff (1822-1894)

The Church's One Foundation

The Church's one Foundation
Is Jesus Christ her Lord;
She is his new creation
By water and the word:
From heav'n he came and sought her
To be his holy Bride;
With his own blood he bought her,
And for her life he died.

Elect from ev'ry nation,
Yet one o'er all the earth,
Her charter of salvation
One Lord, one faith, one birth;
One holy name she blesses,
Partakes one holy food,
And to one hope she presses,

With ev'ry grace endued.

'Mid toil and tribulation,
And tumult of her war,
She waits the consummation
Of peace forevermore;
Till with the vision glorious
Her longing eyes are blest,
And the great Church victorious
Shall be the Church at rest.

Yet she on earth hath union
With God the Three in One,
And mystic sweet communion
With those whose rest is won:
O happy ones and holy!
Lord, give us grace that we,
Like them, the meek and lowly,
On high may dwell with thee.

Samuel J. Stone (1839-1900)

The Old Rugged Cross

O n a hill far away stood an old rugged cross,
The emblem of suffering and shame;
And I love that old cross where the dearest and best
For a world of lost sinners was slain.

Refrain:
  So I'll cherish the old rugged cross,
  'Til my trophies at last I lay down;
  I will cling to the old rugged cross,
  And exchange it someday for a crown.

O that old rugged cross, so despised by the world,
Has a wondrous attraction for me;
For the dear Lamb of God left His glory above
To bear it to dark Calvary.

In the old rugged cross, stained with blood so divine,
A wondrous beauty I see;
For 'twas on that old cross Jesus suffered and died
To pardon and sanctify me.

To the old rugged cross I will ever be true,
It's shame and reproach gladly bear;
Then He'll call me someday to my home far away,
Where His glory forever I'll share.

George Bennard *(1873-?)*

What A Friend We Have In Jesus

What a Friend we have in Jesus,
    All our sins and griefs to bear!
What a privilege to carry
Everything to God in prayer!
O what peace we often forfeit,
O what needless pain we bear,
All because we do not carry
Ev'rything to God in prayer!

Have we trials and temptations?
Is there trouble anywhere?
We should never be discouraged:
Take it to the Lord in prayer!
Can we find a friend so faithful,
Who will all our sorrows share?
Jesus knows our every weakness—
Take it to the Lord in prayer!

Are we weak and heavy-laden,
Cumbered with a load of care?
Precious Saviour, still our Refuge,
Take it to the Lord in prayer!

Do thy friends despise, forsake thee?
Take it to the Lord in prayer!
In his arms he'll take and shield thee,
Thou wilt find a solace there.

Joseph Scriven (1820-1886)

When I Survey the Wondrous Cross

When I survey the wondrous cross
On which the Prince of Glory died,
My richest gain I count but loss,
And pour contempt on all my pride.

Forbid it, Lord, that I should boast,
Save in the death of Christ my God;
All the vain things that charm me most,
I sacrifice them to his blood.

See, from his head, his hands, his feet,
Sorrow and love flow mingled down:
Did e'er such love and sorrow meet,
Or thorns compose so rich a crown?

Were the whole realm of nature mine,
That were a present far too small;
Love so amazing so divine,
Demands my soul, my life, my all.

Isaac Watts (1674-1748)

More Favorites

More Favorites

More Favorites

More Favorites

More Favorites

Part Four

Treasured Scriptures

Treasures From the Old Testament

A nd God saw everything that he had made, and, be-hold, *it was* very good.

Genesis 1:31

AND GOD SAID, This *is* the token of the covenant which I make between me and you and every living creature that is with you, for perpetual generations: I do set my bow in the cloud, and it shall be for a token of a covenant between me and the earth. And it shall come to pass, when I bring a cloud over the earth, that the bow shall be seen in the cloud: And I will remember my covenant, which *is* between me and you and every living creature of all flesh; and the waters shall no more become a flood to destroy all flesh.

Genesis 9:12-15

AND THE ANGEL of the LORD called unto Abraham out of heaven the second time, And said, By myself have I sworn, saith the LORD, for because thou hast done this thing, and hast not withheld thy son, thine only *son:* That in blessing I will bless thee, and in multiplying I will multiply thy seed as the stars of the heaven, and as the sand which *is* upon the sea shore; and thy seed shall possess the gate of his enemies; And in thy seed shall all the nations of the earth be blessed; because thou hast obeyed my voice.

Genesis 22:15-18

GIVE EAR, O ye heavens, and I will speak; and hear, O earth, the words of my mouth. My doctrine shall drop as the rain, my speech shall distil as the dew, as the small rain upon the tender herb, and as the showers upon the grass: Because I will publish the name of the LORD: ascribe ye greatness unto our God. *He is* the Rock, his work is perfect: for all his ways *are* judgment: a God of truth and without iniquity, just and right *is* he.

Deuteronomy 32:1-4

HAVE NOT I commanded thee? Be strong and of a good courage; be not afraid, neither be thou dismayed: for the LORD thy God *is* with thee whithersoever thou goest.

Joshua 1:9

CHOOSE YOU THIS day whom ye will serve....but as for me and my house, we will serve the LORD.

Joshua 24:15

AND RUTH SAID, Intreat me not to leave thee, or to return from following after thee: for whither thou goest, I will go; and where thou lodgest, I will lodge: thy people *shall be* my people, and thy God my God.

Ruth 1:16

ONLY FEAR THE LORD, and serve him in truth with all your heart: for consider how great *things* he hath done for you.

1 Samuel 12:24

BE STRONG AND of good courage, and do it: fear not, nor be dismayed: for the LORD God, even my God, will be with thee; he will not fail thee, nor forsake thee, until thou hast finished all the work for the service of the house of the LORD.

1 Chronicles 28:20

WHEREFORE DAVID blessed the LORD before all the congregation: and David said, Blessed *be* thou, LORD God of Israel our father, for ever and ever. Thine, O LORD, *is* the greatness, and the power, and the glory, and the victory, and the majesty: for all *that is* in the heaven and in the earth *is thine;* thine *is* the kingdom, O LORD, and thou art exalted as head above all. Both riches and honour *come* of thee, and thou reignest over all; and in thine hand is power and might; and in thine hand *it is* to make great, and to give strength unto all. Now therefore, our God, we thank thee, and praise thy glorious name.

1 Chronicles 29:10-13

IF MY PEOPLE, which are called by my name, shall humble themselves, and pray, and seek my face, and turn from their wicked ways; then will I hear from heaven, and will forgive their sin, and will heal their land.

2 Chronicles 7:14

Treasures From the Prophets

Thou wilt keep him in perfect peace, whose mind is stayed on thee: because he trusteth in thee.

Isaiah 26:3

BUT THEY THAT wait upon the LORD shall renew their strength; they shall mount up with wings as eagles; they shall run, and not be weary; and they shall walk, and not faint.

Isaiah 40:31

FOR THE MOUNTAINS shall depart, and the hills be removed; but my kindness shall not depart from thee, neither shall the covenant of my peace be removed, saith the LORD that hath mercy on thee.

Isaiah 54:10

SEEK YE THE LORD while he may be found, call ye upon him while he is near.

Isaiah 55:6

BUT NOW, O LORD, thou art our father; we are the clay, and thou our potter; and we all are the work of thy hand.

Isaiah 64:8

AND IT SHALL come to pass, that before they call, I will answer; and while they are yet speaking, I will hear.

Isaiah 65:24

BLESSED IS THE man that trusteth in the LORD, and whose hope the LORD is. For he shall be as a tree planted by the waters, and that spreadeth out her roots by the river, and shall not see when heat cometh, but her leaf shall be green; and shall not be careful in the year of drought, neither shall cease from yielding fruit....I the LORD search the heart, I try the reins, even to give every man according to his ways, and according to the fruit of his doings.

Jeremiah 17:7-8,10

FOR I KNOW the thoughts that I think toward you, saith the LORD, thoughts of peace, and not of evil, to give you an expected end. Then shall ye call upon me, and ye shall go and pray unto me, and I will hearken unto you. And ye shall seek me, and find me, when ye shall search for me with all your heart.

Jeremiah 29:11-13

THE LORD HATH appeared of old...saying, Yea, I have loved thee with an everlasting love: therefore with loving-kindness have I drawn thee.

Jeremiah 31:3

AND THEY SHALL be my people, and I will be their God: And I will give them one heart, and one way, that they may fear me for ever, for the good of them, and of their children after them: And I will make an everlasting covenant with them, that I will not turn away from them, to do them good; but I will put my fear in their hearts, that they shall not depart from me.

Jeremiah 32:38-40

CALL UNTO ME, and I will answer thee, and show thee great and mighty things, which thou knowest not.

Jeremiah 33:3

IT IS OF the LORD'S mercies that we are not consumed, because his compassions fail not. They are new every morning: great is thy faithfulness.

Lamentations 3:22-23

THE LORD IS my portion, saith my soul; therefore will I hope in him. The LORD is good unto them that wait for him, to the soul that seeketh him. It is good that a man should both hope and quietly wait for the salvation of the LORD.

Lamentations 3:24-26

I WILL SEEK that which was lost, and bring again that which was driven away, and will bind up *that which was* broken, and will strengthen that which was sick.

Ezekiel 34:16

THE LORD THY God in the midst of thee is mighty; he will save, he will rejoice over thee with joy; he will rest in his love, he will joy over thee with singing.

Zephaniah 3:17

Treasures From the Psalms

B lessed is the man that walketh not in the counsel of the ungodly, nor standeth in the way of sinners, nor sitteth in the seat of the scornful. But his delight is in the law of the LORD; and in his law doth he meditate day and night. And he shall be like a tree planted by the rivers of water, that bringeth forth his fruit in his season; his leaf also shall not wither; and whatsoever he doeth shall prosper.

Psalm 1:1-3

BUT THOU, O LORD, art a shield for me; my glory, and the lifter up of mine head.

Psalm 3:3

I WILL BOTH lay me down in peace, and sleep; for thou, LORD, only makest me dwell in safety.

Psalm 4:8

MY VOICE SHALT thou hear in the morning, O LORD; in the morning will I direct *my prayer* unto thee, and will look up. Lead me, O LORD, in thy righteousness...make thy way straight before my face....Let all those that put their trust in thee rejoice: let them ever shout for joy, because thou defendest them: let them also that love thy name be joyful in thee. For thou, LORD, wilt bless the righteous; with favour wilt thou compass him as *with* a shield.

Psalm 5:3,8,11-12

THE LORD HATH heard my supplication; the LORD will receive my prayer.

Psalm 6:9

I WILL PRAISE the LORD according to his righteousness: and will sing praise to the name of the LORD most high.

Psalm 7:17

THE LORD ALSO will be a refuge for the oppressed, a refuge in times of trouble. And they that know thy name will put their trust in thee: for thou, LORD, hast not forsaken them that seek thee.

Psalm 9:9-10

THE WORDS OF the LORD *are* pure words: *as* silver tried in a furnace of earth, purified seven times. Thou shalt keep them, O LORD, thou shalt preserve them from this generation for ever.

Psalm 12:6-7

LORD, WHO SHALL abide in thy tabernacle? Who shall dwell in thy holy hill? He that walketh uprightly, and worketh righteousness, and speaketh the truth in his heart.

Psalm 15:1-2

THOU WILT SHEW me the path of life: in thy presence is fulness of joy; at thy right hand *there are* pleasures for evermore.

Psalm 16:11

I WILL LOVE thee, O LORD, my strength. The LORD *is* my rock, and my fortress, and my deliverer; my God, my strength, in whom I will trust; my buckler, and the horn of my salvation, *and* my high tower.

Psalm 18:1-2

WITH THE MERCIFUL thou wilt shew thyself merciful; with an upright man thou wilt shew thyself upright; with the pure thou wilt shew thyself pure; and with the froward thou wilt shew thyself froward. For thou wilt save the afflicted people; but wilt bring down high looks. For thou wilt light my candle: the LORD my God will enlighten my darkness....It is God that girdeth me with strength, and maketh my way perfect. He maketh my feet like hinds' *feet*, and setteth me upon my high places.... The LORD liveth; and blessed be my rock; and let the God of my salvation be exalted.

Psalm 18:25-28,32-33,46

THE LAW OF the LORD *is* perfect, converting the soul: the testimony of the LORD *is* sure, making wise the simple. The statutes of the LORD *are* right, rejoicing the heart: the commandment of the LORD *is* pure, enlightening the eyes. The fear of the LORD *is* clean, enduring for ever: the judgments of the LORD *are* true *and* righteous altogether. More to be desired *are they* than gold, yea, than much fine gold: sweeter also than honey and the honeycomb....Let the words of my mouth, and the meditation of my heart, be acceptable in thy sight, O LORD, my strength, and my redeemer.

Psalm 19:7-10,14

BE THOU EXALTED, LORD, in thine own strength: so will we sing and praise thy power.

Psalm 21:13

THE EARTH IS the LORD'S, and the fulness thereof; the world, and they that dwell therein.

Psalm 24:1

UNTO THEE, O LORD, do I lift up my soul. O my God, I trust in thee: let me not be ashamed, let not mine enemies triumph over me....Shew me thy ways, O LORD; teach me thy paths. Lead me in thy truth, and teach me: for thou *art* the God of my salvation; on thee do I wait all the day. Remember, O LORD, thy tender mercies and thy lovingkindnesses; for they *have been* ever of old. Remember not the sins of my youth, nor my transgressions: according to thy mercy remember thou me for thy goodness' sake, O LORD.

Psalm 25:1-2,4-7

ONE *THING* HAVE I desired of the LORD, that will I seek after; that I may dwell in the house of the LORD all the days of my life, to behold the beauty of the LORD, and to inquire in his temple.... Wait on the LORD: be of good courage, and he shall strengthen thine heart: wait, I say, on the LORD.

Psalm 27:4,14

GIVE UNTO THE LORD, O ye mighty, give unto the LORD glory and strength. Give unto the LORD the glory due unto his name; worship the LORD in the beauty of holiness.

Psalm 29:1-2

BE OF GOOD courage, and he shall strengthen your heart, all ye that hope in the LORD.

Psalm 31:24

I WILL INSTRUCT thee and teach thee in the way which thou shalt go: I will guide thee with mine eye.

Psalm 32:8

BLESSED *IS* THE nation whose God *is* the LORD; *and* the people *whom* he hath chosen for his own inheritance.

Psalm 33:12

I WILL BLESS the LORD at all times: his praise *shall* continually be in my mouth....O magnify the LORD with me, and let us exalt his name together....O taste and see that the LORD *is* good: blessed *is* the man *that* trusteth in him. O fear the LORD, ye his saints: for *there is* no want to them that fear him....Many *are* the afflictions of the righteous: but the LORD delivereth him out of them all.

Psalm 34:1,3,8-9,19

HOW EXCELLENT IS thy lovingkindness, O God! Therefore the children of men put their trust under the shadow of thy wings.

Psalm 36:7

TRUST IN THE LORD, and do good; *so* shalt thou dwell in the land, and verily thou shalt be fed. Delight thyself also in the LORD; and he shall give thee the desires of thine heart. Commit thy way unto the LORD; trust also in him; and he shall being *it* to pass....Rest in the LORD, and wait patiently for him.... Wait on the LORD, and keep his way, and he shall exalt thee to inherit the land.

Psalm 37:3-5,7,34

I WAITED PATIENTLY for the LORD; and he inclined unto me, and heard my cry. He brought me up also out of an horrible pit, out of the miry clay, and set my feet upon a rock, *and* established my goings. And he hath put a new song in my mouth, *even* praise unto our God.

Psalm 40:1-3

WHY ART THOU cast down, O my soul? And why art thou disquieted within me? Hope thou in God: for I shall yet praise him, *who is* the health of my countenance, and my God.

Psalm 42:11

GOD IS OUR refuge and strength, a very present help in trouble. Therefore will not we fear, though the earth be removed, and though the mountains be carried into the midst of the sea; *though* the waters thereof roar *and* be troubled, though the mountains shake with the swelling thereof. Selah. *There is* a river, the streams whereof shall make glad the city of God, the holy *place* of the tabernacles of the most High. God *is* in the midst of her; she shall not be moved: God shall help her, and that right early.... Be still, and know that I *am* God: I will be exalted among the heathen, I will be exalted in the earth.

Psalm 46:1-5,10

CALL UPON ME in the day of trouble: I will deliver thee, and thou shalt glorify me.

Psalm 50:15

HAVE MERCY UPON me, O God, according to thy lovingkindness: according unto the multitude of thy tender mercies blot out my transgressions. Wash me thoroughly from mine iniquity, and cleanse me from my sin....Purge me with hyssop, and I shall be clean: wash me, and I shall be whiter than snow....Create in me a clean heart, O God; and renew a right spirit within me. Cast me not away from thy presence; and take not thy Holy Spirit from me. Restore unto me the joy of thy salvation; and uphold me *with thy* free spirit.

Psalm 51:1-2,7,10-12

EVENING, AND MORNING, and at noon, will I pray, and cry aloud: and he shall hear my voice.

Psalm 55:17

BE THOU EXALTED, O God, above the heavens: *let* thy glory *be* above all the earth.

Psalm 57:11

MY SOUL, WAIT thou only upon God; for my expectation *is* from him. He only *is* my rock and my salvation: he is my defence; I shall not be moved. In God *is* my salvation and my glory: the rock of my strength, *and* my refuge, *is* in God. Trust in him at all times; ye people, pour out your heart before him: God *is* a refuge for us.

Psalm 62:5-8

BECAUSE THOU HAST been my help, therefore in the shadow of thy wings will I rejoice.

Psalm 63:7

MAKE A JOYFUL noise unto God, all ye lands: sing forth the honour of his name: make his praise glorious.

Psalm 66:1-2

BLESSED BE THE Lord, *who* daily loadeth us *with benefits, even* the God of our salvation.

Psalm 68:19

HIS NAME SHALL endure for ever: his name shall be continued as long as the sun: and *men* shall be blessed in him: all nations shall call him blessed.

Psalm 72:17

THOU SHALT GUIDE me with thy counsel, and afterward receive me *to* glory.

Psalm 73:24

I WILL MEDITATE also of all thy work, and talk of thy doings. Thy way, O God, *is* in the sanctuary: who *is so* great a God as *our* God? Thou *art* the God that doest wonders: thou hast declared thy strength among the people.

Psalm 77:12-14

FOR A DAY in thy courts *is* better than a thousand. I had rather be a doorkeeper in the house of my God, than to dwell in the tents of wickedness. For the LORD God *is* a sun and shield: the LORD will give grace and glory: no good *thing* will he withhold from them that walk uprightly.

Psalm 84:10-11

I WILL SING of the mercies of the LORD for ever: with my mouth will I make known thy faithfulness to all generations....Blessed *is* the people that know the joyful sound: they shall walk, O LORD, in the light of thy countenance. In thy name shall they rejoice all the day: and in thy righteousness shall they be exalted. For thou *art* the glory of their strength: and in thy favour our horn shall be exalted.

Psalm 89:1,15-17

SO TEACH US to number our days, that we may apply our hearts unto wisdom.

Psalm 90:12

IT IS A good *thing* to give thanks unto the LORD, and to sing praises unto thy name, O most High: to shew forth thy lovingkindness in the morning, and thy faithfulness every night.

Psalm 92:1-2

O COME, LET us worship and bow down: let us kneel before the LORD our maker. For he *is* our God; and we *are* the people of his pasture, and the sheep of his hand.

Psalm 95:6-7

LET THE HEAVENS rejoice, and let the earth be glad; let the sea roar, and the fulness thereof. Let the field be joyful, and all that *is* therein: then shall all the trees of the wood rejoice before the LORD: for he cometh, for he cometh to judge the earth: he shall judge the world with righteousness, and the people with his truth.

Psalm 96:11-13

BLESS THE LORD, O my soul: and all that is within me, bless his holy name. Bless the LORD, O my soul, and forget not all his benefits: Who forgiveth all thine iniquities; Who healeth all thy diseases; Who redeemeth thy life from destruction; Who crowneth thee with lovingkindness and tender mercies; Who satisfieth thy mouth with good *things;* so that thy youth is renewed like the eagle's.

Psalm 103:1-5

O LORD, HOW manifold are thy works! In wisdom hast thou made them all: the earth is full of thy riches.

Psalm 104:24

PRAISE YE THE LORD. O give thanks unto the LORD; for he is good: for his mercy *endureth* for ever.

Psalm 106:1

OH THAT *MEN* would praise the LORD *for* his goodness, and *for* his wonderful works to the children of men!

Psalm 107:31

THE FEAR OF the LORD *is* the beginning of wisdom: a good understanding have all they that do *his commandments:* his praise endureth for ever.

Psalm 111:10

FROM THE RISING of the sun unto the going down of the same the LORD'S name *is* to be praised.

Psalm 113:3

RETURN UNTO THY rest, O my soul; for the LORD hath dealt bountifully with thee.

Psalm 116:7

IT IS BETTER to trust in the LORD than to put confidence in man. *It is* better to trust in the LORD than to put confidence in princes...I will praise thee: for thou hast heard me, and art become my salvation. The stone *which* the builders refused is become the head *stone* of the corner. This is the LORD'S doing; it *is* marvellous in our eyes. This *is* the day *which* the LORD hath made; we will rejoice and be glad in it.

Psalm 118:8-9,21-24

THY WORD HAVE I hid in mine heart, that I might not sin against thee. Blessed *art* thou, O LORD: teach me thy statutes. With my lips have I declared all the judgments of thy mouth. I have rejoiced in the way of thy testimonies, as *much as* in all riches. I will meditate in thy precepts, and have respect unto thy ways. I will delight myself in thy statutes: I will not forget thy word.... Make me to understand the way of thy precepts: so shall I talk of thy wondrous works....Teach me, O LORD, the way of thy statutes; and I shall keep it *unto* the end. Give me understanding, and I shall keep thy law; yea, I shall observe it with my whole heart....Teach me good judgment and knowledge: for I have believed thy commandments....How sweet are thy words unto my taste! *Yea, sweeter* than honey to my mouth....Thy word is a lamp unto my feet, and a light unto my path.... Thou *art* my hiding place and my shield: I hope in thy word....The entrance of thy words giveth light; it giveth understanding unto the simple....Thy word *is* true *from* the beginning: and every one of thy righteous judgments *endureth* for ever.

Psalm 119:11-16,27,33-34,103,105,114,130,160

THEY THAT SOW in tears shall reap in joy.

Psalm 126:5

THE LORD WILL perfect *that which* concerneth me: thy mercy, O LORD, *endureth* for ever: forsake not the works of thine own hands.

Psalm 138:8

SEARCH ME, O God, and know my heart: try me, and know my thoughts: and see if *there be any* wicked way in me, and lead me in the way everlasting.

Psalm 139:23-24

TEACH ME TO do thy will; for thou *art* my God: thy spirit is good; lead me into the land of uprightness.

Psalm 143:10

THE LORD IS gracious, and full of compassion; slow to anger, and of great mercy.... The LORD *is* nigh unto all them that call upon him, to all that call upon him in truth.

Psalm 145:8,18

PRAISE YE THE LORD: Praise ye the LORD from the heavens: praise him in the heights. Praise ye him, all his angels: praise ye him, all his hosts. Praise ye him, sun and moon: praise him, all ye stars of light. Praise him, ye heavens of heavens, and ye waters that *be* above the heavens.... Kings of the earth, and all people; princes, and all judges of the earth: Both young men, and maidens; old men, and children: Let them praise the name of the LORD: for his name alone is excellent; his glory *is* above the earth and heaven.

Psalm 148:1-4,11-13

Treasures From the Proverbs

The fear of the LORD is the beginning of knowledge: *but* fools despise wisdom and instruction. My son, hear the instruction of thy father, and forsake not the law of thy mother: for they *shall be* an ornament of grace unto thy head, and chains about thy neck.

Proverbs 1:7-9

FOR THE LORD giveth wisdom: out of his mouth *cometh* knowledge and understanding. He layeth up sound wisdom for the righteous: *he* is a buckler to them that walk uprightly.

Proverbs 2:6-7

TRUST IN THE LORD with all thine heart; and lean not unto thine own understanding. In all thy ways acknowledge him, and he shall direct thy paths.

Proverbs 3:5-6

HAPPY *IS* THE man *that* findeth wisdom, and the man *that* getteth understanding: For the merchandise of it is better than the merchandise of silver, and the gain thereof than fine gold. She *is* more precious than rubies: and all the things thou canst desire are not to be compared unto her. Length of days *is* in her right hand; and in her left hand riches and honour. Her ways *are* ways of pleasantness, and all her paths *are* peace. She *is* a tree of life to them that lay hold upon her: and happy *is every one* that retaineth her.

Proverbs 3:13-18

TAKE FAST HOLD of instruction; let *her* not go: keep her; for she *is* thy life....Keep thy heart with all diligence; for out of it *are* the issues of life....Ponder the path of thy feet, and let all thy ways be established.

Proverbs 4:13,23,26

MY SON, KEEP thy father's commandment, and forsake not the law of thy mother: bind them continually upon thine heart, *and* tie them about thy neck. When thou goest, it shall lead thee; when thou sleepest, it shall keep thee; and *when* thou awakest, it shall talk with thee. For the commandment *is* a lamp; and the law *is* light; and reproofs of instruction *are* the way of life.

Proverbs 6:20-23

GIVE *INSTRUCTION* TO a wise man, and he will be yet wiser: teach a just man, and he will increase in learning.

Proverbs 9:9

WHERE NO COUNSEL *is,* the people fall: but in the multitude of counsellers *there* is safety.

Proverbs 11:14

HEAVINESS IN THE heart of man maketh it stoop: but a good word maketh it glad.

Proverbs 12:25

COMMIT THY WORKS unto the LORD, and thy thoughts shall be established.

Proverbs 16:3

PLEASANT WORDS *ARE as* an honeycomb, sweet to the soul, and health to the bones.

Proverbs 16:24

A FRIEND LOVETH at all times, and a brother is born for adversity.

Proverbs 17:17

THE NAME OF the LORD *is* a strong tower: the righteous runneth into it, and is safe.

Proverbs 18:10

A MAN *THAT hath* friends must shew himself friendly: and there is a friend *that* sticketh closer than a brother.

Proverbs 18:24

COUNSEL IN THE heart of man *is like* deep water; but a man of understanding will draw it out.

Proverbs 20:5

THE SPIRIT OF man *is* the candle of the LORD, searching all the inward parts of the belly.

Proverbs 20:27

EVERY WORD OF God *is* pure: he *is* a shield unto them that put their trust in him.

Proverbs 30:5

The Wife Of Noble Character

A wife of noble character who can find?
  She is worth far more than rubies.
Her husband has full confidence in her
  and lacks nothing of value.
She brings him good, not harm,
  all the days of her life.
She selects wool and flax
  and works with eager hands.
She is like the merchant ships,
  bringing her food from afar.
She gets up while it is still dark;
  she provides food for her family

and portions for her servant girls.
She considers a field and buys it;
  out of her earnings she plants a vineyard.
She sets about her work vigorously;
  her arms are strong for her tasks.
She sees that her trading is profitable,
  and her lamp does not go out at night.
In her hand she holds the distaff
  and grasps the spindle with her fingers.
She opens her arms to the poor
  and extends her hands to the needy.
When it snows, she has no fear for
  her household; for all of them are clothed in scarlet.
She makes coverings for her bed;
  she is clothed in fine linen and purple.
Her husband is respected at the city gate,
  where he takes his seat among the
  elders of the land.
She makes linen garments and sells them,
  and supplies the merchants with sashes.
She is clothed with strength and dignity;
  she can laugh at the days to come.
She speaks with wisdom,
  and faithful instruction is on her tongue.
She watches over the affairs of her household
  and does not eat the bread of idleness.
Her children arise and call her blessed;
  her husband also, and he praises her:
"Many women do noble things,
  but you surpass them all."

Charm is deceptive, and beauty is fleeting;
  but a woman who fears the LORD is
  to be praised.
Give her the reward she has earned,
  and let her works bring her praise
  at the city gate.

Proverbs 31:10-31 (NIV)

The Christmas Story

And it came to pass in those days, that there went out a decree from Caesar Augustus, that all the world should be taxed. (*And* this taxing was first made when Cyrenius was governor of Syria.) And all went to be taxed, every one into his own city.

And Joseph also went up from Galilee, out of the city of Nazareth, into Judea, unto the city of David, which is called Bethlehem; (because he was of the house and lineage of David:) To be taxed with Mary his espoused wife, being great with child.

And so it was, that, while they were there, the days were accomplished that she should be delivered. And she brought forth her firstborn son, and wrapped him in swaddling clothes, and laid him is a manger; because there was no room for them in the inn.

And there were in the same country shepherds abiding in the field, keeping watch over their flock by night. And, lo, the angel of the Lord came upon them, and the glory of the Lord shone round about them: and they were sore afraid.

And the angel said unto them, Fear not: for, behold, I bring you good tidings of great joy, which shall be to all people.

For unto you is born this day in the city of David a Savior, which is Christ the Lord. And this *shall be* a sign unto you; Ye shall find the babe wrapped in swaddling clothes, lying in a manger.

And suddenly there was with the angel a multitude of the heavenly host praising God, and saying,

Glory to God in the highest,
and on earth peace,
good will toward men.

And it came to pass, as the angels were gone away from them into heaven, the shepherds said one to another, Let us now go even unto Bethlehem, and see this thing which is come to pass, which the Lord hath made known unto us.

And they came with haste, and found Mary, and Joseph, and the babe lying in a manger.

And when they had seen *it*, they made known abroad the saying which was told them concerning this child. And all they that heard *it* wondered at those things which were told them by the shepherds.

But Mary kept all these things, and pondered them in her heart.

And the shepherds returned, glorifying and praising
God for all the things that they had heard and seen, as it
was told unto them.

Luke 2:1-20

Treasures From the Words Of Christ

L et your light so shine before men, that they may see
your good works, and glorify your Father which is
in heaven.

Matthew 5:16

LOVE YOUR ENEMIES, bless them that curse you, do
good to them that hate you, and pray for them which de-
spitefully use you, and persecute you; That ye may be the
children of your Father which is in heaven: for he maketh
his sun to rise on the evil and on the good, and sendeth
rain on the just and on the unjust.

Matthew 5:44-45

BUT THOU, WHEN thou prayest, enter into thy closet,
and when thou hast shut thy door, pray to thy Father
which is in secret; and thy Father which seeth in secret
shall reward thee openly.

Matthew 6:6

LAY NOT UP for yourselves treasures upon earth, where
moth and rust doth corrupt, and where thieves break

through and steal: But lay up for yourselves treasures in heaven, where neither moth nor rust doth corrupt, and where thieves do not break through nor steal: For where your treasure is, there will your heart be also.

Matthew 6:19-21

NO MAN CAN serve two masters: for either he will hate the one, and love the other; or else he will hold to the one, and despise the other. Ye cannot serve God and mammon.

Matthew 6:24

ASK, AND IT shall be given you; seek, and ye shall find; knock, and it shall be opened unto you: For every one that asketh receiveth; and he that seeketh findeth; and to him that knocketh it shall be opened.

Matthew 7:7-8

The Golden Rule

THEREFORE ALL things whatsoever ye would that men should do to you, do ye even so to them.

Matthew 7:12

ENTER YE IN at the strait gate: for wide is the gate, and broad is the way, that leadeth to destruction, and many there be which go in thereat: Because strait is the gate, and narrow is the way, which leadeth unto life, and few there be that find it.

Matthew 7:13-14

ACCORDING TO YOUR faith be it unto you.

Matthew 9:29

THE HARVEST TRULY *is* plenteous, but the labourers *are* few; Pray ye therefore the Lord of the harvest, that he will send forth labourers into his harvest.

Matthew 9:37-38

ARE NOT TWO sparrows sold for a farthing? and one of them shall not fall on the ground without your Father. But the very hairs of your head are all numbered. Fear ye not therefore, ye are of more value than many sparrows. Whosoever therefore shall confess me before men, him will I confess also before my Father which is in heaven. But whosoever shall deny me before men, him will I also deny before my Father which is in heaven....He that findeth his life shall lose it: and he that loseth his life for my sake shall find it.

Matthew 10:29-33,39

The Great Invitation

COME UNTO ME, all ye that labor and are heavy laden, and I will give you rest. Take my yoke upon you, and learn of me; for I am meek and lowly in heart: and ye shall find rest unto your souls. For my yoke is easy, and my burden is light.

Matthew 11:28-30

OUT OF THE abundance of the heart the mouth speaketh.

Matthew 12:34

IF ANY MAN will come after me, let him deny himself, and take up his cross, and follow me. For whosoever will save his life shall lose it: and whosoever will lose his life for my sake shall find it. For what is a man profited, if he shall gain the whole world, and lose his own soul? or what shall a man give in exchange for his soul?

Matthew 16:24-26

IF YE HAVE faith as a grain of mustard seed, ye shall say unto this mountain, Remove hence to yonder place; and it shall remove; and nothing shall be impossible unto you.

Matthew 17:20

VERILY I SAY unto you, Except ye be converted, and become as little children, ye shall not enter into the kingdom of heaven. Whosoever therefore shall humble himself as this little child, the same is greatest in the kingdom of heaven. And whoso shall receive one such little child in my name receiveth me.

Matthew 18:3-5

FOR THE SON of man is come to save that which was lost. How think ye? If a man have an hundred sheep, and one of them be gone astray, doth he not leave the ninety and nine, and goeth into the mountains, and seeketh that which is gone astray? And if so be that he find it, verily I say unto you, he rejoiceth more of that *sheep*, than of the ninety and nine which went not astray. Even so it is not the will of your Father which is in heaven, that one of these little ones should perish.

Matthew 18:11-14

SUFFER LITTLE CHILDREN, and forbid them not, to come unto me: for of such is the kingdom of heaven.

Matthew 19:14

WHATSOEVER YE SHALL ask in prayer, believing, ye shall receive.

Matthew 21:22

HEAVEN AND EARTH shall pass away, but my words shall not pass away. But of that day and hour knoweth no *man*, no, not the angels of heaven, but my Father only.... Watch therefore: for ye know not what hour your Lord doth come.

Matthew 24:35,36,42

I SAY UNTO thee, Except a man be born again, he cannot see the kingdom of God....Except a man be born of water and of the Spirit, he cannot enter into the kingdom of God. That which is born of the flesh is flesh; and that which is born of the Spirit is spirit. Marvel not that I said unto thee, Ye must be born again. The wind bloweth where it listeth, and thou hearest the sound thereof, but canst not tell whence it cometh, and whither it goeth: so is every one that is born of the Spirit.

John 3:3,5-8

FOR GOD SO loved the world, that he gave his only begotten Son, that whosoever believeth in him should not perish, but have everlasting life. For God sent not his Son into the world to condemn the world; but that the world through him might be saved.

John 3:16-17

BUT WHOSOEVER DRINKETH of the water that I shall give him shall never thirst; but the water that I shall give him shall be in him a well of water springing up into everlasting life.

John 4:14

GOD *IS* A Spirit: and they that worship him must worship *him* in spirit and in truth.

John 4:24

SEARCH THE SCRIPTURES; for in them ye think ye have eternal life: and they are they which testify of me.

John 5:39

I AM THE bread of life: he that cometh to me shall never hunger; and he that believeth on me shall never thirst.... Verily, verily, I say unto you, He that believeth on me hath everlasting life.

John 6:35,47

IF THE SON therefore shall make you free, ye shall be free indeed.

John 8:36

I AM THE good shepherd: the good shepherd giveth his life for the sheep.... I am the good shepherd, and know my *sheep*, and am known of mine.

John 10:11,14

I AM THE resurrection, and the life: he that believeth in me, though he were dead, yet shall he live: And whosoever liveth and believeth in me shall never die.

John 11:25-26

AND I, IF I be lifted up from the earth, will draw all *men* unto me.... I am come a light into the world, that whosoever believeth on me should not abide in darkness.

John 12:32,46

A NEW COMMANDMENT I give unto you, That ye love one another; as I have loved you, that ye also love one another. By this shall all men know that ye are my disciples, if ye have love one to another.

John 13:34-35

ABIDE IN ME, and I in you. As the branch cannot bear fruit of itself, except it abide in the vine; no more can ye, except ye abide in me. I am the vine, ye *are* the branches: He that abideth in me, and I in him, the same bringeth forth much fruit: for without me ye can do nothing.... If ye abide in me, and my words abide in you, ye shall ask what ye will, and it shall be done unto you. Herein is my Father glorified, that ye bear much fruit; so shall ye be my disciples. As the Father hath loved me, so have I loved you: continue ye in my love.... These things have I spoken unto you, that my joy might remain in you, and that your joy might be full.

John 15:4-5,7-9,11

YE SHALL RECEIVE power, after that the Holy Ghost is come upon you: and ye shall be witnesses unto me both in Jerusalem, and in all Judea, and in Samaria, and unto the uttermost part of the earth.

Acts 1:8

BEHOLD, I STAND at the door and knock: if any man hear my voice, and open the door, I will come in to him, and will sup with him, and he with me.

Revelation 3:20

I AM ALPHA and Omega, the beginning and the end, the first and the last.

Revelation 22:13

The Twelve Disciples

A nd when he had called unto *him* his twelve disciples, he gave them power *against* unclean spirits, to cast them out and to heal all manner of sickness and all manner of disease.

Now the names of the twelve apostles are these; The first, Simon, who is called Peter, and Andrew his brother; James *the son* of Zebedee, and John his brother;

Philip, and Bartholomew; Thomas, and Matthew the publican; James *the son* of Alphaeus, and Lebbaeus, whose surname was Thaddaeus;

Simon the Canaanite, and Judas Iscariot, who also betrayed him.

Matthew 10:1-4

The Great Commandment

J esus said unto him,
Thou shalt love the Lord thy God with all thy heart, and with all thy soul, and with all thy mind.
This is the first and great commandment.
And the second is like unto it,
Thou shalt love thy neighbor as thyself.
On these two commandments hang all the law and the
prophets.

Matthew 22:37-40

The Great Commission

And Jesus came and spake unto them, saying, All power is given unto me in heaven and in earth. Go ye therefore, and teach all nations, baptizing them in the name of the Father, and of the Son, and of the Holy Ghost: Teaching them to observe all things whatsoever I have commanded you: and, lo, I am with you always, even unto the end of the world. Amen.

Matthew 28:18-20

From the Comfort Chapter

Let not your heart be troubled: ye believe in God, believe also in me.

In my Father's house are many mansions: if *it were* not so, I would have told you. I go to prepare a place for you.

And if I go and prepare a place for you, I will come again, and receive you unto myself; that where I am, *there* ye may be also.

If ye love me, keep my commandments.

And I will pray the Father, and he shall give you another Comforter, that he may abide with you forever.

Peace I leave with you, my peace I give unto you: not as the world giveth, give I unto you. Let not your heart be troubled, neither let it be afraid.

John 14:1-3,15-16,27

The Love Chapter

If I speak in the tongues of men and of angels, but have not love, I am only a resounding gong or a clanging cymbal. If I have the gift of prophecy and can fathom all mysteries and all knowledge, and If I have a faith that can move mountains, but have not love, I am nothing. If I give all I possess to the poor and surrender my body to the flames, but have not love, I gain nothing.

Love is patient, love is kind. It does not envy, it does not boast, it is not proud. It is not rude, it is not self-seeking, it is not easily angered, it keeps no record of wrongs. Love does not delight in evil but rejoices with the truth. It always protects, always trusts, always hopes, always perseveres.

Love never fails. But where there are prophecies, they will cease; where there are tongues, they will be stilled; where there is knowledge, it will pass away. For we know in part and we prophesy in part, but when perfection comes, the imperfect disappears. When I was a child, I talked like a child, I thought like a child, I reasoned like a child. When I became a man, I put childish ways behind me. Now we see but a poor reflection; then we shall see face to face.

Now I know in part; then I shall know fully, even as I am fully known.

And now these three remain: faith, hope and love. But the greatest of these is love.

1 Corinthians 13 (NIV)

The Fruit Of the Spirit

The fruit of the Spirit is love, joy, peace, patience, kindness, goodness, faithfulness, gentleness and self-contol. Against such things there is no law.

Galations 5:22-23 (NIV)

The Gifts Of the Spirit

Now about spiritual gifts, brothers, I do not want you to be ignorant. You know that when you were pagans, somehow or other you were influenced and led astray to dumb idols. Therefore I tell you that no one who is speaking by the Spirit of God says, "Jesus be cursed," and no one can say, "Jesus is Lord," except by the Holy Spirit.

There are different kinds of gifts, but the same Spirit. There are different kinds of service, but the same Lord. There are different kinds of working, but the same God works all of them in all men.

Now to each one the manifestation of the Spirit is given for the common good. To one there is given through the Spirit the message of wisdom, to another the message of knowledge by means of the same Spirit, to another faith by the same Spirit, to another gifts of healing by that one Spirit, to another miraculous powers, to another prophecy, to another the ability to distinguish between spirits, to another the ability to speak in different kinds of tongues, and to still another the interpretation of tongues.

All these are the work of one and the same Spirit, and he gives them to each man, just as he determines.

1 Corinthians 12:1-11 (NIV)

The Armour Of God

B e strong in the Lord, and in the power of his might. Put on the whole armour of God, that ye may be able to stand against the wiles of the devil. For we wrestle not against flesh and blood, but against principalities, against powers, against the rulers of the darkness of this world, against spiritual wickedness in high *places*.

Wherefore take unto you the whole armour of God, that ye may be able to withstand in the evil day, and having done all, to stand.

Stand therefore, having your loins girt about with truth, and having on the breastplate of righteousness; And your feet shod with the preparation of the gospel of peace; Above all, taking the shield of faith, wherewith ye shall be able to quench all the fiery darts of the wicked. And take the helmet of salvation, and the sword of the Spirit, which is the word of God: Praying always with all prayer and supplication in the Spirit, and watching thereunto with all perseverance and supplication for all saints.

Ephesians 6:10-18

Treasures From the New Testament Writers

In the beginning was the Word, and the Word was with God, and the Word was God. The same was in the beginning with God. All things were made by him; and without him was not any thing made that was made. In him was life; and the life was the light of men. And the light shineth in darkness; and the darkness comprehended it not.

John 1:1-5

FOR I AM not ashamed of the gospel of Christ: for it is the power of God unto salvation to every one that believeth....For therein is the righteousness of God revealed from faith to faith: as it is written, The just shall live by faith.

Romans 1:16-17

FOR ALL HAVE sinned, and come short of the glory of God.

Romans 3:23

THEREFORE BEING justified by faith, we have peace with God through our Lord Jesus Christ: By whom also we have access by faith into this grace wherein we stand, and rejoice in hope of the glory of God. And not only *so*, but we glory in tribulations also: knowing that tribulation worketh patience; And patience, experience; and experience, hope: And hope maketh not ashamed; because the love of God is shed abroad in our hearts by the Holy Ghost which is given unto us.

Romans 5:1-5

FOR THE WAGES of sin *is* death; but the gift of God *is* eternal life through Jesus Christ our Lord.

Romans 6:23

FOR AS MANY as are led by the Spirit of God, they are the sons of God.

Romans 8:14

FOR I AM persuaded, that neither death, nor life, nor angels, nor principalities, nor powers, nor things present, nor things to come, nor height, nor depth, nor any other creature, shall be able to separate us from the love of God, which is in Christ Jesus our Lord.

Romans 8:38-39

FOR WITH THE heart man believeth unto righteousness; and with the mouth confession is made unto salvation....For whosoever shall call upon the name of the Lord shall be saved....So then faith cometh by hearing, and hearing by the word of God.

Romans 10:10,13,17

I BESEECH YOU therefore, brethren, by the mercies of God, that ye present your bodies a living sacrifice, holy, acceptable unto God, which is your reasonable service.

And be not conformed to this world: but be ye trans-
formed by the renewing of your mind, that ye may prove
what is that good, and acceptable, and perfect, will of
God.

Romans 12:1-2

NOW WE HAVE received, not the spirit of the world,
but the spirit which is of God; that we might know the
things that are freely given to us of God.

1 Corinthians 2:12

KNOW YE NOT that ye are the temple of God, and
that the Spirit of God dwelleth in you?

1 Corinthians 3:16

FOR THE KINGDOM of God is not in word, but in
power.

1 Corinthians 4:20

THERE HATH NO temptation taken you but such as is
common to man: but God is faithful, who will not suffer
you to be tempted above that ye are able; but will with
the temptation also make a way to escape, that ye may be
able to bear it.

1 Corinthians 10:13

THEREFORE, MY BELOVED brethren, be ye stedfast, unmoveable, always abounding in the work of the Lord, forasmuch as ye know that your labour is not in vain in the Lord.

1 Corinthians 15:58

THEREFORE IF ANY man be in Christ, he is a new creature: old things are passed away; behold, all things are become new.

2 Corinthians 5:17

HE WHICH SOWETH sparingly shall reap also sparingly; and he which soweth bountifully shall reap also bountifully. Every man according as he purposeth in his heart, *so let him give*; not grudgingly, or of necessity: for God loveth a cheerful giver. And God *is* able to make all grace abound toward you; that ye, always having all sufficiency in all *things*, may abound to every good work.

2 Corinthians 9:6-8

MY GRACE IS sufficient for thee: for my strength is made perfect in weakness. Most gladly therefore will I rather glory in my infirmities, that the power of Christ may rest upon me.

2 Corinthians 12:9

THE JUST SHALL live by faith.

Galations 3:11

IF WE LIVE in the Spirit, let us also walk in the Spirit.

Galations 5:25

BE NOT DECEIVED; God is not mocked: for whatsoever a man soweth, that shall he also reap.

Galations 6:7

FOR BY GRACE are ye saved through faith; and that not
of yourselves: *it is* the gift of God: Not of works, lest any
man should boast. For we are his workmanship, created
in Christ Jesus unto good works, which God hath before
ordained that we should walk in them.

Ephesians 2:8-9

AND BE RENEWED in the spirit of your mind; And
that ye put on the new man, which after God is created
in righteousness and true holiness.

Ephesians 4:23-24

BE YE THEREFORE followers of God, as dear children; And walk in love, as Christ also hath loved us, and
hath given himself for us an offering and a sacrifice to
God for a sweetsmelling savour.

Ephesians 5:1-2

BUT BE FILLED with the Spirit; Speaking to yourselves
in psalms and hymns and spiritual songs, singing and
making melody in your heart to the Lord; Giving thanks
always for all things unto God and the Father in the name

of our Lord Jesus Christ; Submitting yourselves one to another in the fear of God.

Ephesians 5:18-21

FINALLY, MY BRETHREN, be strong in the Lord, and in the power of his might.

Ephesians 6:10

BEING CONFIDENT OF this very thing, that he which hath begun a good work in you will perform *it* until the day of Jesus Christ.

Philippians 1:6

THAT AT THE name of Jesus every knee should bow.... And that every tongue should confess that Jesus Christ is Lord, to the glory of God the Father.

Philippians 2:10-11

THIS ONE THING *I do,* forgetting those things which are behind, and reaching forth unto those things which are before, I press toward the mark for the prize of the high calling of God in Christ Jesus.

Philippians 3:13-14

REJOICE IN THE Lord alway: and again I say, Rejoice. Let your moderation be known unto all men. The Lord *is* at hand. Be careful for nothing; but in every thing by prayer and supplication with thanksgiving let your requests be made known unto God. And the peace of

God, which passeth all understanding, shall keep your hearts and minds through Christ Jesus.

Philippians 4:4-7

FINALLY, BRETHREN, whatsoever things are true, whatsoever things are honest, whatsoever things are just, whatsoever things are pure, whatsoever things are lovely, whatsoever things are of good report; if there be any virtue, and if there be any praise, think on these things.

Philippians 4:8

I CAN DO all things through Christ which strengtheneth me.

Philippians 4:13

BUT MY GOD shall supply all your need according to his riches in glory by Christ Jesus.

Philippians 4:19

AS YE HAVE therefore received Christ Jesus the Lord, so walk ye in him: Rooted and built up in him, and stablished in the faith, as ye have been taught, abounding therein with thanksgiving.

Colossians 2:6-7

LET THE WORD of Christ dwell in you richly in all wisdom; teaching and admonishing one another in psalms and hymns and spiritual songs, singing with grace in your hearts to the Lord. And whatsoever ye do in word or deed, do all in the name of the Lord Jesus, giving thanks to God and the Father by him.

Colossians 3:16-17

REJOICE EVERMORE. Pray without ceasing. In every thing give thanks: for this is the will of God in Christ Jesus concerning you.

1 Thessalonians 5:16-18

STUDY TO SHOW thyself approved unto God, a workman that needeth not to be ashamed, rightly dividing the word of truth.

2 Timothy 2:15

ALL SCRIPTURE IS given by inspiration of God, and is profitable for doctrine, for reproof, for correction, for instruction in righteousness: That the man of God may be perfect, thoroughly furnished unto all good works.

2 Timothy 3:16-17

I HAVE FOUGHT a good fight, I have finished *my* course, I have kept the faith: Henceforth there is laid up for me a crown of righteousness, which the Lord, the righteous judge, shall give me at that day: and not to me only, but unto all them also that love his appearing.

2 Timothy 4:7-8

FOR THE WORD of God is quick, and powerful, and sharper than any twoedged sword, piercing even to the dividing asunder of soul and spirit, and of the joints and marrow, and *is* a discerner of the thoughts and intents of the heart.

Hebrews 4:12

CAST NOT AWAY therefore your confidence, which hath great recompence of reward. For ye have need of patience, that, after ye have done the will of God, ye might receive the promise.

Hebrews 10:35-36

NOW FAITH IS the substance of things hoped for, the evidence of things not seen.

Hebrews 11:1

BUT WITHOUT FAITH it is impossible to please him: for he that cometh to God must believe that he is, and that he is a rewarder of them that diligently seek him.

Hebrews 11:6

IF ANY OF you lack wisdom, let him ask of God, that giveth to all men liberally, and upbraideth not; and it shall be given him.

James 1:5

EVERY GOOD AND every perfect gift is from above, and cometh down from the Father of lights, with whom there is no variableness, neither shadow of turning.

James 1:17

SUBMIT YOURSELVES therefore to God. Resist the devil, and he will flee from you. Draw nigh to God, and he will draw nigh to you.

James 4:7-8

THE EFFECTUAL FERVENT prayer of a righteous man availeth much.

James 5:16

AS HE WHICH hath called you is holy, so be ye holy in all manner of conversation; Because it is written, Be ye holy; for I am holy.

1 Peter 1:15-16

YE ARE A chosen generation, a royal priesthood, an holy nation, a peculiar people; that ye should shew forth the praises of him who hath called you out of darkness into his marvellous light.

1 Peter 2:9

GOD RESISTETH THE proud, and giveth grace to the humble. Humble yourselves therefore under the mighty hand of God, that he may exalt you in due time: Casting all your care upon him; for he careth for you.

1 Peter 5:5-7

ADD TO YOUR faith virtue; and to virtue knowledge; And to knowledge temperance; and to temperance patience; and to patience godliness; And to godliness brotherly kindness; and to brotherly kindness charity.

2 Peter 1:5-7

THE LORD IS not slack concerning his promise, as some men count slackness; but is longsuffering to us-ward, not willing that any should perish, but that all should come to repentance.

2 Peter 3:9

GROW IN GRACE, and *in* the knowledge of our Lord and Saviour Jesus Christ. To him *be* glory both now and for ever.

2 Peter 3:18

IF WE WALK in the light, as he is in the light, we have fellowship one with another, and the blood of Jesus Christ his Son cleanseth us from all sin. If we say that we have no sin, we deceive ourselves, and the truth is not in us. If we confess our sins, he is faithful and just to forgive us our sins, and to cleanse us from all unrighteousness.

1 John 1:7-9

BEHOLD, WHAT MANNER of love the Father hath bestowed upon us, that we should be called the sons of God.

1 John 3:1

HEREIN IS LOVE, not that we loved God, but that he loved us, and sent his Son to be the propitiation for our sins.

1 John 4:10

THERE IS NO fear in love; but perfect love casteth out fear.

1 John 4:18

AND THIS IS the confidence that we have in him, that, if we ask anything according to his will, he heareth us: And if we know that he hear us, whatsoever we ask, we know that we have the petitions that we desired of him.

1 John 5:14-15

AND THIS IS love, that we walk after his commandments.

2 John:6

BELOVED, I WISH above all things that thou mayest prosper and be in health, even as thy soul prospereth....I have no greater joy than to hear that my children walk in truth.

3 John:2-4

BUT YE, BELOVED, building up yourselves on your most holy faith, praying in the Holy Ghost, Keep yourselves in the love of God, looking for the mercy of our Lord Jesus Christ unto eternal life.

Jude:20-21

BEHOLD, I COME quickly: hold that fast which thou hast, that no man take thy crown.

Revelation 3:11

EVEN SO, COME, Lord Jesus.

Revelation 22:20

More Favorites

More Favorites

More Favorites

More Favorites

Acknowledgments

We gratefully acknowledge use of the following material:

The poems "Four Things to Do," The Zest Of Life," "These Are the Gifts I ask," from *The Poems of Henry van Dyke*, Rev. Edn. (New York: Charles Scribner's Sons, 1920). Used by permission.

The poem "The Secret" by Ralph Spaulding Cushman from *Spiritual Hilltops* (Nashville: Abingdon Press). Used by permission.

The poem "If I Can" by Emily Dickinson from *The Complete Poems of Emily Dickinson* (Boston: Little, Brown and Company). Used by permission.

The poem "Proof" by Ethel Romig Fuller from *Kitchen Sonnets*. (Portland, OR: Binford & Mort Publishing). Used by permission.

The prayer "For This Universe" by Walter Rauschenbusch from *Prayers of the Social Awakening* by Walter Rauschenbusch. (New York: Pilgrim Press, 1910). Used by permission.

Index

Other **Evergreen** titles you won't want to miss:

Time Out! A Men's Devotional
Compiled by Clint and Mary Beckwith

Songs From the Heart
Compiled by Mary Beckwith

Help For Hurting Moms
By Kathy Collard Miller

What Believers Must Know to Grow
By Tom Carter

Please check with your local bookstore or write us for more information on how you may obtain these and other **Evergreen** titles:

Evergreen Communications, Inc.
2085-A Sperry Avenue
Ventura, CA 93003

Or phone:

(805) 650-9248